SUPER TIPS FOR SUPER MEMORY

Sushant Mysorekar completed his education in educational and career counselling and psychology. He has over fifteen years of experience in training, mentoring and research in the field of Cognition and Intelligence, and has been certified by the Institute of Psychological Health. Awarded the 'Gold Medalist Master Trainer' in Musical Windows Memorization Systems used globally, he is an internationally acclaimed master trainer and cognitive therapist in the field of memory who has coached regular and differently abled students and professionals in more than fifteen countries.

He has received the Excellence Award by the Asia-Africa Development Council, India, and the University of Mumbai for his contributions in the field of education. As the chief secretary of Indian Memory Sports Council, India, he promotes and organizes school and national-level memory championships in India as well as abroad. He is renowned for his counselling skills and memory optimization methods that have helped his students excel in innovation and creativity.

SUPER TIPS FOR SUPER MEMORY

Sushant Mysorekar

RUPA

Published by
Rupa Publications India Pvt. Ltd 2019
7/16, Ansari Road, Daryaganj
New Delhi 110002

Sales Centres:

Allahabad Bengaluru Chennai
Hyderabad Jaipur Kathmandu
Kolkata Mumbai

Copyright © Sushant Mysorekar 2019

The views and opinions expressed in this book are the
author's own and the facts are as reported by him which
have been verified to the extent possible, and the publishers
are not in any way liable for the same.

All rights reserved.
No part of this publication may be reproduced, transmitted,
or stored in a retrieval system, in any form or by any means,
electronic, mechanical, photocopying, recording or otherwise,
without the prior permission of the publisher.

ISBN: 978-93-5333-350-8

First impression 2019

10 9 8 7 6 5 4 3 2 1

The moral right of the author has been asserted.

Printed by Nutech Print Services, Faridabad

This book is sold subject to the condition that it shall not,
by way of trade or otherwise, be lent, resold, hired out, or otherwise
circulated, without the publisher's prior consent, in any form of binding or
cover other than that in which it is published.

Contents

Foreword | vii

1. Know Yourself | 1
2. About Brain | 20
3. How to Develop Good Memory | 32
4. Learning Style | 39
5. Right and Left Brain | 53
6. Brain-Mind-Memory | 63
7. United Method | 76
8. Creativity | 89
9. Multiple Methods | 94
10. Focus and Concentration | 104
11. Vedic Maths | 113
12. Brain Mapping | 124
13. Vocabulary Builder | 128
14. Stress | 143
15. Meditation and Relaxation | 148
16. Emotional Freedom Techniques (EFTs) | 161
17. Musical Windows | 166
18. Thinking Skills | 181
19. Boost Your Brain Power | 190

Conclusion | 198

Acknowledgements | 199

Foreword

It is with great pleasure and a sense of purpose that I write this preamble to what I truly endorse as a keepsake book. The author, Sushant Mysorekar, has been in a close professional association with me, hence, I am aware of his ethos and thought process to a great extent. I took on this enriching task because it ignited in me a researcher, biochemist and above all, an academician.

Mysorekar has arranged his penmanship in a chequered journey, where the reader is taken through the answers of why, what, when, which and, finally, how to address the native question of memory consolidation and, of course, value addition of arguably the most precious and nodal organ of the body—the brain. The chapters are flavoured with a distinct undertone of experience and the first-hand knowledge of the author which makes the reading worthwhile. In fact, one is tempted to take notes and mull over various paragraphs with great interest, and the exercises act as a catalyst, which tempt the reader to embark on an exciting adventure of the mind. The author has been very perceptive in recognizing how the mind of the young reader—the student—is made up. Hence, the informality of language and ease of thought make up for receptive reading.

It is said that life is a wonderful and constant teacher, but it is for those who wish to learn. If one were to divide life into various compartmentalized aspects, the one which could be described as most exciting, vibrant and vivid would be none other than the time in a student's life. Armed with the vigour and energy of youth and equipped with an undying sense of optimism, the student days are often described by many as the 'golden years'. Indeed, anthropologists have observed that the totality of the quality of life is measured by the manner in which the years of studentship have been spent by an individual. The main reason for this is that the manner in which self-enhancement can be accomplished during these days. Knowledge-gleaning, attaining wisdom and building up of an empathy quotient are all investments toward a sustainable holistic betterment. Memory 'protection' and brain health are two veritable tools towards this endeavour.

This book is relevant and timeless as it addresses these issues of universal relevance with great detail and in a systematic and focussed manner. I thoroughly enjoyed this literary journey and am grateful to the author for his creativity. I recommend the reader to enjoy this work in an exhaustive and introspective manner. It will definitely result in self-enrichment.

'Self-love, self-respect, self-worth—there is a reason that all these start with the word "self"... They do not belong to anyone but you!'

Happy reading and congratulations, Sushantji!

Dr Jyoti D. Vora
MSc, PhD, FSSc, MASFFBC, CME (USA),
Certified Functional Foods Scientist (FFC, USA),
CEO of Dhirang Consultants, Mumbai

Chapter 1

Know Yourself

1.1: Introduction

Congratulations! You are one of the amazing mental athletes who has taken a powerful first step in knowing, learning and adopting the tools, techniques and systems to understand how the brain functions. In the course of reading this book, you will learn how to navigate your ship (body) successfully in the vast ocean (the world) with the help of resources (mind, memory, thoughts, etc.) to reach your goals. Trust me; once you have mastered this truly valuable skill of memorizing, you will never want to remember anything the 'hard' way!

This book will help you effortlessly remember information that will boost your career, skyrocket your grades and save yourself the sheer inconvenience of storing loads of information.

Let me share with you my story.

I was very poor in studies, struggled hard to clear my exams and could only move on to the next class with grace marks. I somehow completed my graduation in BSc (Chemistry) from Ruparel College, Matunga. It was then that I started my journey in the corporate world. I worked for a few years in various companies and in different departments. I always felt that there was something missing, but I could not identify what it was.

Coincidentally, with the help of my sister, Sulbha Vaidya, I happened to meet the first mentor of my life, Dilip Tikle, who identified the real me. He gave me an opportunity to work under his able guidance as a counsellor in MET, Mumbai. A few years later, he introduced me to someone without whom I could not have even existed in the field of Memory.

Vikrant Chaphekar is a simple man with a charismatic personality, full of energy and enthusiasm. He guides students to excel in their field with the help of his knowledge and experience. He is a true innovator, creator, mentor and a fatherly figure, lovingly known as Vikrant Dada by trainers, parents and students all over the globe. After my training, I conducted my first-ever paid programme at Yash Infotech, Byculla, with about eight students under his guidance. It was then that my journey on the path of memory training began.

A few years later, in 2009, while conducting a memory session at Help Library, where I would conduct one session every month, I met Francis Xavier from Bangalore—an 82-year-old dynamic personality, who offered me to work with him. My journey with Xavier started, and together, we conducted programmes in Mumbai, Pune, Chennai, Hyderabad and Kolkata. We nurtured around 250 memory trainers.

With confidence in Mind, Brain and Memory, I went to UAE, where I conducted live sessions. I was also invited to Egypt as a strategic partner for conducting the School Memory Championship and the first International Conference on Memory.

In my journey ahead, I met another mastermind in creativity, innovations, learning, braindancer, author and presenter, Dilip Mukerjea from Singapore, who again helped me achieve higher levels in memory training. The thought process and learning acquired with the millennial generation helped me create more tools and techniques suitable for today's needs. His ideas and creative visuals used during a session and the way he spoke mesmerized me; this made me reach out to him frequently.

It is because of the support of my mentors and my family

that I have been able to write this book.

Now, before we proceed with detailed information, knowledge and learning about the brain, let's assess our understanding and working of your present memory.

Let us form a belief system, which can help us nurture our children and make them better human beings:

- Our belief that school and parents are equal partners in the development of a child, and that a relationship between the two is based on understanding, trust and sensitivity, is of paramount importance in achieving our common goal of our children's all-round development.
- We believe that every child is unique and has certain qualities that are special, irrespective of his or her level of intelligence and natural ability. It is our duty to trust each child, and treat him or her with love and care so that he or she grows up into a good human being with high self-esteem.
- Since children have different talents and interests, we, as parents, guide, friend, mentor or anyone for that matter, should provide equal opportunity, environment and freedom to pursue activities that suit their individual interests and abilities.
- A child's first role model is his or her parents. During their early years, children learn more from elders. Therefore, we should lay great emphasis on the right conduct of the teachers at the child's school, parents at home and guides at their respective institutions. We should also urge the community we live in to set the right example before the children.
- We should be committed to excellence in everything we do and should strive to inculcate the same habit in our

children, too. They will grow up to become our country's future leaders.
- Today's children are no different from those in the past. The only difference is the available resources and tools. Gadgets, apps and software have made learning interesting. Therefore, we should consider it our responsibility to find ways and means to make the learning experience interesting for our children.
- We believe in developing the overall personality of a child. It is also our responsibility to understand his or her level of intelligence and nurture them to build social awareness, high self-esteem and confidence. He or she must be encouraged and enabled to participate in sports, arts, literature and other areas.

The journey from '**to-be**' to '**have-become**' is a process.

Various assessments, such as Strength–Weakness–Opportunities–Threat analysis (SWOT), Biometric analysis, Attention, Memory and Frontal Abilities Screening Test (AMFAST) etc., provide you an insight into the talents acquired from birth, skills learned and goals achieved. Before undergoing a memory programme, you need to travel through the journey of your life and understand the difference between what you were earlier and how this programme will transform your journey to create a new you.

Introspecting about your inner self is of prime importance. We all have tremendous potential, but since we have not been evaluated on such terms during the early stages of life, we are not aware of our inborn potential. This book shall help you know yourself better—assess your inherent abilities, efficiently use creative and logical abilities, understand the use of individual compartments in your brain, activate brain cells and put them to proper use, identify individual learning styles and patterns, multiple intelligences and strengths. All of these can be developed by learning and applying certain systems, tools and techniques that are being used globally and have been useful to many. All of us are born geniuses; however, the secrets to channelize and activate the cells remain unknown to many or have not been researched earlier. This book is my attempt to show you how all of us can have super memories and excel at work and in life.

Let us begin with an **assessment** of what this programme can offer and make you aware of your loopholes and pitfalls.

1.2: Assessment

Aim: To help you reflect on your knowledge, learning and understanding of the subject before undergoing this programme.

Learning objective: To analyse your working knowledge about the potentials of your brain.

What you need: Presence of mind, a pencil or a pen, an eraser.

What needs to be done: Take a moment to go through the questionnaire below and indicate your views and opinions on the given questions.

Once you assess yourself, you can decide whether you are required to undertake any Brain Development Training Programme (BDTP). This programme shall help you to master the required skills. You can mail us the filled assessment sheet on our email id: info@brainrhyme.com.

With growing needs, we are in the process of starting Brain Learning Centres at different locations that shall not only provide training but also help students in academics, design certain tools based on learning styles and follow-ups with students for their overall development. On completion of the programme, each student shall be awarded a certificate which is globally recognized.

Let us start!

Tick wherever applicable:

Gender: ☐ Male   ☐ Female
Age Group: ☐ Less than 10   ☐ 10-18   ☐ 19-25
☐ 25 & above

1. Learn how brain and memory work together for better performance.
   ☐ I need to know   ☐ I have a bit of an idea   ☐ I know
2. Do you know how to be organized?
   ☐ I need to learn   ☐ I have a bit of an idea   ☐ I know
3. Do you know which learning style suits you best?
   ☐ I need to know   ☐ I have a bit of an idea   ☐ I know
4. Do you know your working style?
   ☐ I need to know   ☐ I have a bit of an idea   ☐ I know
5. Do you know how to recall 70–80 per cent of what you have read?
   ☐ I need to know   ☐ I have a bit of an idea   ☐ I know
6. Do you know how to read at the speed of 600–800 words per minute?
   ☐ I need to know   ☐ I have a bit of an idea   ☐ I know
7. Do you know how to map information for easy understanding and recalling abilities?
   ☐ I need to know   ☐ I have a bit of an idea   ☐ I know
8. Do you know how to calculate logical problems mentally?
   ☐ I need to know   ☐ I have a bit of an idea   ☐ I know
9. Do you know how to remember regularly used words at the tip of the tongue?
   ☐ I need to know   ☐ I Have a bit of an idea   ☐ I know
10. Do you remember what you hear and see, read directions,

people's names, locations, stories, novels, educational content, etc.?

Hear ☐ I need to learn ☐ I have a bit of an idea ☐ I know
See ☐ I need to learn ☐ I have a bit of an idea ☐ I know
Read ☐ I need to learn ☐ I have a bit of an idea ☐ I know

11. Do you know the art of observation and focussed attention?
    ☐ I need to know ☐ I Have a bit of an idea ☐ I know
12. Do you know the process and art of conversation?
    ☐ I need to know ☐ I have a bit of an idea ☐ I know
13. Do you know the art of listening to sounds, music, etc., clearly and accurately?
    ☐ I need to know ☐ I have a bit of an idea ☐ I know
14. Do you have the knack for identifying faces?
    ☐ I need to know ☐ I have a bit of an idea ☐ I know
15. Do you know the art of reading information with speed, accuracy and understanding (magazines, articles, newspapers, books, etc.)?
    ☐ I need to know ☐ I Have a bit of an idea ☐ I know
16. Have you learned the art of curiosity?
    ☐ I need to know ☐ I have a bit of an idea ☐ I know
17. Are you aware of the thinking and decision-making process?
    ☐ I need to know ☐ I have a bit of an idea ☐ I know
18. Are you creative? Have you tested your creativity?
    ☐ I need to know ☐ I have a bit of an idea ☐ I know
19. Do you know smart learning methods?
    ☐ I need to know ☐ I have a bit of an idea ☐ I know
20. Do you know the process to learn, unlearn and relearn?
    ☐ I need to know ☐ I have a bit of an idea ☐ I know

Now, assess yourself. If you have marked,

☐ **I need to know or learn,** it means that you are ready to learn and that you wish to improve on your skills. You are about to take the first step in improving your memory skills.

- ☐ **I have a bit of an idea,** it means that you are aware of some aspects but are not sure how they are going to help you. However, you are ready to learn and improve your memory skills.

- ☐ **I know,** it means that you are aware of some techniques, systems, etc. You have either learned it or have undergone a brain development-training programme.

Thank you very much for taking this test.

Now, let's go through your academic journey. Analyse yourself and fill the following questionnaire.

1.3: Questionnaire

The following questionnaire is specially designed to help you understand the present and future generation methodologies of using the brain's effectiveness. Survey questionnaires are a part of several academic study councils in India and abroad. Please answer the following questions:

Academic subjects:

1. How do you study?

   _____
   _____
   _____

2. What are the methods you adopt to memorize long answers?

   _____
   _____
   _____

3. What happens during exams?

   _____
   _____
   _____

4. What academic skills do you think you have?
   a) _____
   b) _____
   c) _____
5. What academic skills do you think you should have in future?
   a) _____
   b) _____
   c) _____
6. Which are the top three skills that you think toppers possess?
   a) _____
   b) _____
   c) _____

Reading:

Answer the following questions and introspect your reading skills.

1. Do you agree that reading is a skill and should be taught in school?
   ☐ Yes   ☐ No
2. What is your reading speed? If you are not sure how to calculate, follow the instructions below:
   - Take a book of your choice. Time your reading to 2 minutes and read the way you usually do. STOP reading after two minutes.
   - Count the number of words you have read and divide it by 2. For example, if you have read 100 words in 2 minutes, divide the number by 2, i.e., 50 words per minute. Your reading speed is 50 words per minute.

3. How do you read? (You may select multiple options.)
   a) Read silently
   b) Read aloud
   c) Read with music on
   d) Read with fingers on the text
   e) Read with hand movements
4. What percentage of the content can you recall after reading it once? (select one)
   a) 100 per cent
   b) Between 90–100 per cent
   c) Between 80–90 per cent
   d) Between 70–80 per cent
   e) Less than 70 per cent
5. How many times do you need to read to understand at least 90 per cent of what you have read?
   a) Only once
   b) Twice
   c) Thrice
   d) More than three times
6. Name three benefits of knowing how to read.
   a) _____
   b) _____
   c) _____
7. How many books do you read in…
   a) One month: _____
   b) Three months: _____
   c) Six months: _____
   d) One year: _____
8. What type of books do you prefer reading? (You may select multiple options.)
   a) Only text
   b) With coloured images and symbols

- c) Cartoon characters
- d) Story format
- e) Magazines
- f) Journals

9. You prefer to read from…
    - a) Book
    - b) Kindle
    - c) Mobile

10. You like to… (You may select multiple options.)
    - a) Read
    - b) Listen
    - c) Participate in debates and discussions
    - d) Chat on WhatsApp, Facebook, etc.

Memory:

1. Your memory is…
    - a) Excellent
    - b) Good
    - c) Poor
    - d) Very Poor

2. Do you face difficulty in all the subjects?
    - a) Yes
    - b) No

3. Which subjects can you retain best?
    - a) _____
    - b) _____
    - c) _____

4. Which subjects can you not retain very well?
    - a) _____
    - b) _____
    - c) _____

5. What are the top three skills you should possess to improve

your memory?
a) _____
b) _____
c) _____

1.4: Myths About Yourself

Based on your academic results or remarks from your teachers, parents, relatives, society and surroundings, you create a self-image. Now, let's see what kind of an image you draw about yourself.

You must honestly accept what you feel about yourself. What you are about to learn and experience shall change your perspective of looking at yourself.

1. I am not good at studies.
2. I am not able to recall answers.
3. I am unable to concentrate or focus on a certain thing.
4. I am not creative.
5. I am not intelligent.
6. My memory is very poor.
7. I am unable to recall numbers.
8. I find it difficult to remember names and faces of people.
9. I find it difficult to remember dates and events.
10. My concentration level is very weak.
11. I believe that I shall not be able to score high marks.
12. My calculation is poor.
13. I think I have a learning disability.
14. I lack the potential to understand things quickly.
15. I cannot recite numbers.
16. I forget the road I last travelled on.
17. I am unable to read quickly.
18. I don't know the benefits of yoga and meditation.

Know Yourself • 13

If you have these misconceptions in your mind, you are about to experience a journey in the course of which your thought process will be clearer and you shall start believing in yourself.

However, you have to participate actively in all the activities in your journey towards having a trained mind with an immense potential for success.

1.5: How to Make the Maximum Utilization of Each Session in This Book

Before the session:

Purpose: Clarify your purpose to take up the training programme.
Prepare: Before coming for the session, prepare yourself for the topic to be discussed. Browse through the Internet, books, articles, etc.

During the session:

Engage: Be present, listen actively, understand the viewpoint of the speaker and participate. Turn into a curious child.
Question: Note down the important information in a creative way that is also easy to understand. Question your curiosity.
Takeaway: What is the one thing that you have learned during the session? Mark them in a different colour, if required.
Review: What is the one valuable thing you had and how are you going to apply it in your day-to-day activities?

After the session:

Plan: Develop a plan to put the new skills, knowledge or insights into action. PRACTISE! PRACTISE! PRACTISE!
Action: Apply what you've learned ASAP! How can I convert the learning into something valuable? Often the best way to learn is

to share or teach what you have just learned.

Celebrate: You need to accept and appreciate yourself and try self-motivation, i.e., congratulate yourself or get yourself a sweet or a gift that you love.

1.6: Are You a Smart Learner or a Fast Learner?

We are all different in terms of our thinking, emotional balance, feelings about ourselves and others, attributes that we inherently possess or learn and habits that we acquire. We are judged at every moment of our lives and we need to prove our capabilities. Our abilities are tested and graded as per results. In fact, the adage, 'Survival of the fittest', is universally accepted. Now, we need to determine whether we fall in the 'right' category or the 'left' category of learners.

Think about the attributes and mark the category that you think fits you.

A smart learner	A fast learner
Knows the answer	Asks questions
Is interested	Is highly curious
Is attentive	Is mentally and physically involved
Has good ideas	Has vivid, silly ideas
Works hard consistently	Plays around, yet performs well
Collects information	Discusses in details, elaborates
Top group	Beyond the group
Listens with interest	Shows strong feelings and opinions
Learns with ease	Researches details well
Needs more than 5 repetitions	Requires just few repetitions to master
Understands ideas	Constructs abstractions
Enjoys peers	Prefers discussions with adults
Grasps meanings	Draws inferences from experiences

Completes assignments	Initiates new ideas
Is receptive	Is intense
Copies accurately	Creates a new design
Enjoys school	Enjoys learning
Absorbs information	Manipulates information
Technician	Inventor, researcher
Good memorizer	Good analyser
Enjoys straightforward, sequential	Thrives on complexity
Is alert	Is a keen observer
Happy with own learning	Is highly self-critical

1.7: Learning Process

Learning starts with the ability to acquire knowledge of new concepts with interest. The gap between a person's ability to learn and his or her capability needs to be filled. Learning is a step-by-step process where students actively participate and thrive to acquire the best possible concepts in a limited time, as well as try to accurately learn the concepts.

Step 1: Getting ready

A student needs to be ready to learn. Being prepared is the first step in any learning process.

Step 2: Explanation of concepts (gaining knowledge)

The teacher or facilitator reads and explains the concept through different tools such as reading, whiteboard, apps, etc.

Step 3: Understanding

The student acquires what is being taught and interprets the information based on his/her learning, knowledge and wisdom.

Step 4: Two-way communication (question and answer)

Students raise questions and sort answers on issues that are not clear, and the facilitator explains the issues in a simpler manner.

Step 5: Input (often clues)

Based on the explanation received from the facilitator, the student creates his own understanding of the topic based on his experience, learning and adaptability.

Step 6: Creating his or her own ideas

One can learn the concept based on the above two factors—understanding (as explained in step 3) and inputs (as explained in step 5)—given by the brain.

Step 7: Processing of information

Our brain processes the information based on internal and external factors such as interest, time, duration to process information, adaptability, disturbance, acceptability, learning, exchange of knowledge, environment and the importance of the subject he or she is learning.

Step 8: Learning through a system

How we learn is based on how the brain captures the information, processes and understands it based on what we have experienced in the past and achieved in the present.

Step 9: Practice or repetition

Learning and practising helps the student to prepare for examinations.

Step 10: Confidence

The more the student adopts Step 8, the more confident he or she becomes.

Step 11: Recall

The ability to understand all the above steps and practise them leads to better recall and comprehension. Overconfidence and excess of stress kill creativity and the ability to think logically, resulting in poor performance.

Now, the question that arises is, which STEPS does a student find difficult to apply? Also, what are the SUBJECTS that students have trouble scoring high marks or credits in? Once we are able to identify the right step, it can help us perform better and increase productivity.

1.7.1: Analysis

Let us assume that a student, Anil, who is studying in class 8, is good at Science, but finds a few subjects difficult. One of these subjects is Math. Let us analyse Anil on the factors above and find the missing link.

Learning Process	Science	Maths
Step 1: Getting ready		
Step 2: Explanation of concepts (gaining knowledge)		
Step 3: Understanding		
Step 4: Two-way communication		
Step 5: Input (often clues)		
Step 6: Creating his or her own ideas		
Step 7: Processing of information		
Step 8: Learning through a system		
Step 9: Practice or repetition		
Step 10: Confidence		
Step 11: Recall		

1.7.2: Observations

Anil is not able to understand the concepts taught in the classroom. He adopts a certain way to process information and get the desired results. In spite of practising, he is unable to connect the synapse, i.e., the missing link so that he remembers what he has learned so far, which is affecting his confidence. Hence, during examinations, he is not able to process the neurons and finds it difficult to recall formulae, processes, steps, etc.

1.7.3: Results

Due to his inability to perform in exams, Anil creates a mindset of not being able to process the information in future as well. Despite performing better in other subjects, Anil was still not able to improve his performance in Math. He may soon lose interest in learning the subject, resulting in a dislike and failure to learn better.

1.8: Activity

Now, do this activity for yourself and check the missing link. Write the names of your subjects in the following row under 'Subjects'.

Analyse for yourself and introspect about the subjects in which you are not able to establish the link. In the course of reading this book, you will learn techniques, methods and systems to overcome the challenges.

Learning Process	Subjects				
Ideas or concepts (gaining knowledge)					
Understanding					
Two-way communication (questions and answers)					

Input (often clues)					
Creating ideas					
Processing information					
Practice or repetition					
Confidence					
Recall					

Notes:

_____
_____
_____
_____

1.9: Summary

Summarize what you have understood from this chapter—your takeaways—and how you would use it daily.

Chapter 2

About Brain

2.1: Introduction

Let us first understand how the 'brain' operates and how it is linked with the Mind, Body and Memory.

- The brain has an extremely complex network of cells called neurons.
- The brain consists of billions of neurons.
- The neurons send information in the form of electrical signals, as well as emotions and feelings in the form of chemical signals to another neuron, and the information is held via a bridge called the synapse.

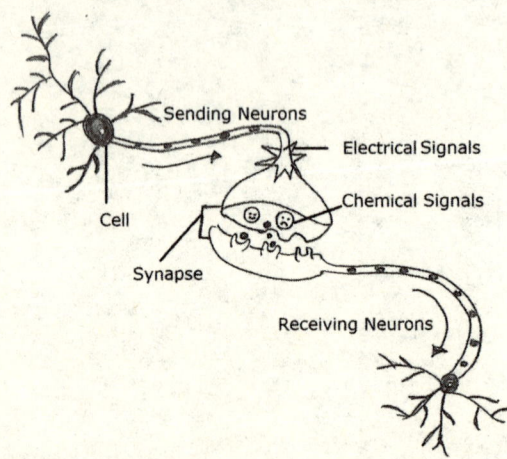

- When any information is acquired, the neurons collect the information and store it for future use with the help of the synapse.

In the above diagram, the information is stored either in the form of electrical signals (verbal communication) or chemical signals (emotions).

There are three types of memory where information is stored.

- Short-term Memory (STM),
- Mid-term Memory (MTM) or
- Long-term Memory (LTM).

Depending upon the attention span and interest in learning, the information is stored in their respective memories. Here are some other facts about the brain you should know:

- The weight of the human brain is about 3 lbs.
- The cerebrum is the largest part of the brain and makes up for 85 per cent of the brain's weight.
- The brain is made up of about 75 per cent water.
- Your brain uses 20 per cent of the total oxygen in your body.
- There are about 1,000 to 10,000 synapses for each neuron.
- Your brain stops growing at age 18.
- Humans continue to make new neurons throughout their lives according to their mental activity.
- Reading aloud and talking often to a young child promote brain development.
- The first sense a baby develops in utero is the sense of touch. The lips and cheeks can experience touch at about eight weeks and the rest of the body around twelve weeks.
- If your brain continues to lose blood for eight to ten seconds, you will lose consciousness.

- While you are awake, your brain generates 10–23 watts of power, or in other words, enough energy to power a light bulb.
- The neocortex makes up about 76 per cent of the human brain and is responsible for language and consciousness.
- The brain can live for four to six minutes without oxygen, and then it begins to die.
- Every time you recall a memory or have a new thought, you are creating a new connection in your brain.
- Memory is formed by associations; so if you want help remembering things, create associations for yourself.
- A study indicates that learning new things helps the brain to develop very quickly.
- Laughing at a joke is no simple task, as it requires five different areas of the brain to work together.
- The Harvard Brain Tissue Resource Center (HBTRC) maintains a Brain Bank, which is a centralized resource for the collection and distribution of human brain specimen for brain research.
- Music lessons considerably boost brain organization in both children and adults.
- The front portion of corpus callosum (the part of the brain that bridges the two halves) is about 11 per cent larger in left-handed or ambidextrous people.

2.2: Brain Layout

The **largest part** of the brain is called the **cerebral cortex**. It is divided into lobes, each of which has a specific function. Most of the processing of information occurs in the cerebral cortex.

The largest part of the cerebral cortex is the **neocortex**. It is divided into four major lobes: the frontal lobe, the parietal lobe, the temporal lobe and the occipital lobe (**F-POT**).

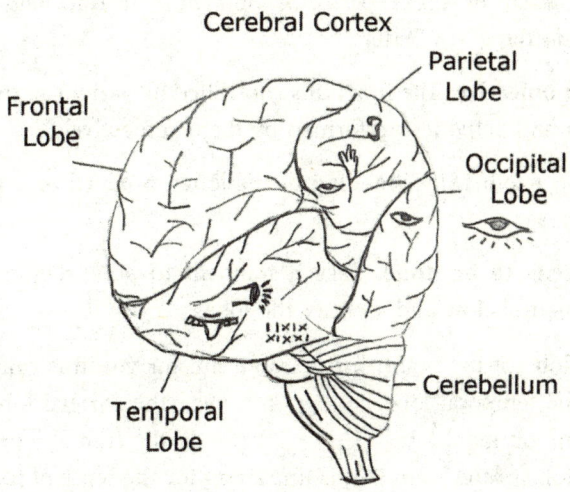

- The **frontal lobe** helps in speaking, planning, comparing and abstract thinking.
- The **parietal lobe** stores visuals, auditory and touch information.
- The **occipital lobe** is the back of the brain that helps to store information related to sight.
- The **temporal lobe** helps in comprehension, sound and speech.

The **cerebrum** is the most highly developed part of the human brain and is responsible for thinking, perceiving, understanding words, increasing vocabulary and understanding language.

2.2.1: Activity: brain lobes

Aim:

To understand the different parts of the brain and the various

24 • *Super Tips for Super Memory*

activities each of them performs and how it can help us understand ourselves better.

Learning objective: The functions controlled by various parts of the brain and activities performed by them respectively.

What you need: Understanding of the lobes, a pencil or a pen and an eraser.

What needs to be done: Take a moment to go through the questionnaire below and identify the lobes:

1. The lobe of the brain that is important for vision is called:
   a. the temporal lobe
   b. the occipital lobe
   c. the parietal lobe
   d. the frontal lobe
2. The lobe of the brain that is important for the sense of touch is called:
   a. the temporal lobe
   b. the occipital lobe
   c. the parietal lobe
   d. the frontal lobe
3. The lobe of the brain that is important for hearing is called:
   a. the temporal lobe
   b. the occipital lobe
   c. the parietal lobe
   d. the frontal lobe
4. The lobe of the brain that is important for reasoning is called:
   a. the temporal lobe
   b. the occipital lobe
   c. the parietal lobe
   d. the frontal lobe
5. The lobe on the diagram shown with eye symbol is:
   a. the temporal lobe
   b. the occipital lobe
   c. the parietal lobe
   d. the frontal lobe
6. The lobe on the diagram shown with eye, hand and ear symbol is:
   a. the temporal lobe
   b. the occipital lobe
   c. the parietal lobe
   d. the frontal lobe
7. The lobe on the diagram shown in sound symbol is:
   a. the temporal lobe
   c. the parietal lobe

b. the occipital lobe	d. the frontal lobe
8. The lobe on the diagram shown with nerve cells is:
   a. the temporal lobe	c. the parietal lobe
   b. the occipital lobe	d. the frontal lobe
9. An adult brain weighs approximately:
   a. 1 lb	c. 5 lbs
   b. 3 lbs	d. 7 lbs
10. A person's brain is about the size of:
    a. their heart	c. 1 fist
    b. their stomach	d. 2 fists

2.3: Mental Functions: Regions

Researchers have found that if you spell out a single word, for instance, 'India', the neurons in a certain part of the brain is activated. It has been observed that various mental functions are localized to different regions of the brain in the following way.

The left part of the brain signals location, words related to 'India', its meaning and the category it belongs to. The right part of the brain signals images of movements, locations and activities related to the word 'India'. Various mental functions are localized to different regions in the following way.

Thinking	Perceptions	Emotions	Behaviour
Communication, planning, comparison, comprehension, processing, reading, focussing, memory	Eyes–See, Ears–Hear, Nose–Smell, Tongue–Taste, Skin–Touch	Happiness, calm, peace, joy, care, sadness, guilt, shame, anger, frustration, worry, fear, nervousness, loneliness, discouragement	Sitting, running, walking, talking, listening, joking, working, playing

Unconscious	Signalling	Intellectual	Emotional
Respiratory system, circulatory system, nervous system, digestive system, musculoskeletal system	Danger, body signals like fatigue, tension, sensory perception	Comparisons, thinking, caution	Fun, romance, parental love

Sentiment		
Hope, happiness		

2.3.1: Activity: Mental functions

Aim: To identify mental functions localized in different regions.

Learning objective: Differentiate the mental functions and categorize into different brain regions. The brain can identify and create awareness about the mental functions and react to the situations accordingly.

What you need: Presence of mind, awareness, a pencil or a pen and an eraser.

What needs to be done: Take a moment to go through the questionnaire below and identify the mental functions:

Talking to a stranger: _____
Studying before examinations: _____
Celebrations—birthdays: _____
Caring nature of parents for their children: _____
Passing comments on others: _____
Feelings for our loved ones: _____
Feeling uneasy after eating too much: _____
Being more creative: _____
Frightened of something: _____
Watching a movie: _____

2.4: Brain Usage

Learning is a continuous process where we acquire new information while **memory** is where we store information for a period of time. Most of the information is acquired from our day-to-day learning. We learn the faces of our parents, siblings, language, numerical calculations, body language, behaviour, etc. We are what we have learned and remember today. Memory is the **glue** that connects life events together.

Humans, normally, have a tendency to use their brain only when needed. We do not make a conscious effort and it has not been practised or taught. We only tend to use the powers of our brain when we are challenged or when you need to think about a certain problem. Unfortunately, we have not been taught the functions of the brain and its capabilities to grasp information and the speed with which it can reproduce.

2.4.1: Activity: Consciousness

Aim: To be conscious in your behaviour, movements, understanding and actively participate.

Learning objective: Awareness of what has been learned and stored and the ability to recall better.

What you need: Presence of mind, a pencil or a pen and an eraser.

What needs to be done: After you read a book, sit for a while in a relaxed position and try this out. Take a break of five minutes for every thirty minutes of work. Close your eyes and try to visualize what you have read. This will help you nourish your brain cells and retain information **because** you do not learn by simply stuffing information into short-term memory. You learn something when you consciously try to store information. This information then connects, or associates, with what you already know (your past experiences, expectations from life, etc.). These short breaks help in making these connections stronger.

2.5: Action

- Pay conscious attention to the activities you do regularly.
- Make a quick note in your mind and visualize the image.
- Note down data, information, news and similar things in order to develop a habit.
- Visualize and create vivid and funny images or exaggerate the activities in terms of images, words or actions so that they stick in your mind for easy recall.
- Link, associate or connect information you wish to recall with objects, names, character, location and create a mental picture as if it is happening right now, right here.

2.6: Where is Memory Stored in the Brain?

German anatomist and physiologist Franz Joseph Gall (1758–1828) found out that mental functions are biological and arise from the brain. French surgeon Paul Broca demonstrated the existence of a speech centre in the brain (1861). Gall was the first to identify the gray matter of the brain with active tissue (neurons) and the white matter with conducting tissue (ganglia). Scientists, today, have found that a personality trait is not localized in any one area of the brain. Different parts of the brain have different functions, but the parts interact in a more complex way.

At its minimum, it involves **vision** (processing and story visual information), **spatial** sense (understanding of shape, size, position, direction and movement), **olfactory** (the sense of smell) and **kinaesthetic** (awareness of the position and movement of the parts of the body by means of sensory organs).

2.7: Theory of Language

Encoded: **Broca's Area**

Broca's area, or the **Broca area,** is a region in the **frontal lobe** of the dominant **hemisphere**, usually the left, of the **brain** with functions linked to **speech production**.

Learning takes place when **the Wernicke's area—region** of the brain that is important for language development—gets activated. It is located in the temporal lobe on the left side of the brain and is responsible for the comprehension of speech, while **Broca's area** is related to the production of speech, i.e, **understanding** of knowledge.

Left Area

- Representation of all languages (including sign language) happens in the left brain
- Broca's area—produces words and signs
- Wernicke's area—(Wernicke's area, also called Wernicke's speech area, is one of the two parts of the cerebral cortex that is linked to speech [the other is Broca's area])—Recognizes words and signs

Right Area

- Broca's equivalent—expresses emotions by intonation
- Wernicke's area—comprehends information
- When we speak, we communicate emotions

If you hear someone speak or read a text, that text is encoded and passed down to the Broca's area, where the understanding of knowledge occurs. Then, the information is passed to the Broca's area, where the grammar is stored.

2.8: Brain Quiz

Level I: Basic

Let us check how many puzzles you are able to recognize.

The first one has been done for your reference and understanding.

24 H in a D: 24 **Hours** in a **Day**

Level II: Advance

Let us check how many you are able to crack:

Level I:

1. 24 H in a D : _____
2. 12 M in a Y = _____
3. 7 D of the W = _____
4. 29 D in a L Y = _____
5. 365 D in a Y = _____
6. 52 W in a Y = _____
7. 60 M in a H = _____

Level II:

8. 7 W of the W = _____
9. 26 L of the A = _____
10. 12 S of the Z = _____
11. 66 B of the B = _____
12. 18 H on a G C = _____
13. 11 P in a F T = _____
14. 13 is U F S = _____
15. 64 S on a C B = _____
16. 15 P in a R T = _____
17. 9 L of a C = _____

18. 1000 Y in a M = _____

Answers:

Level I:
1. 24 Hours in a Day
2. 12 Months in a Year
3. 7 Days in a Week
4. 29 Days in a Leap Year
5. 365 Days in a Year
6. 52 Weeks in a Year
7. 60 Minutes in a Hour.

Level II:
8. 7 Wonders of the World
9. 26 Letters of the Alphabet
10. 12 Signs of the Zodiac
11. 66 Books in the Bible (change from 'of' to 'in')
12. 18 holes on a golf course
13. 11 players in a football team
14. 13 stripes in the US flag
15. 64 squares on a chess board
16. 15 players in a rugby team
17. 9 lives of a cat

2.9: Summary

Summarize what you have understood from this chapter—your takeaways—and how you would use it daily.

Chapter 3

How to Develop Good Memory

3.1: What is Good Memory?

Most of the students fail to understand that good memory is based on several factors: whether you have learned the art of memorizing, what are the methods through which you can learn certain things. IQ is not the only factor to decide how intelligent you are. Your IQ gives a rough indication of your intelligence in terms of knowledge acquired, learning and your instant recall capability.

There are two main aspects to develop a good memory: interest and attention.

Interest is the mother of memory and attention is the father. If you are interested in a particular subject, you shall pay attention, and if you pay conscious attention, it shall help you to memorize what has been discussed.

3.2: Necessity for Developing Memory

In this challenging world, one needs to acquire the skill sets required in the twenty-first century. At every step in life, one faces challenges to learning, exploring, connecting, debating, recalling facts and presenting them in a better and more understandable manner.

Memory is a skill. There are only two types of Memory—Trained and Untrained. An untrained mind and brain is just like shepherds moving in a farm without any proper direction or instruction. Since the art of understanding, articulating, remembering and recalling has not been understood properly, students fail to learn concepts and blame their memory.

This is not true. To develop a good memory, one needs to learn the techniques, methods and then the ability to reproduce when required. A developed memory is just like a rocket ready to launch on one's command. There are no limits to the speed, capacity or destination where it can reach. It is purely how one practises the art and how skilfully they use it for work or in life.

3.3: Basic Principles of Memory

1. *Interest:* Our brain cells capture the information or help us get involved in those things that are of interest to them. Interest can be acquired by forceful involvement based on the subject matter. Interest is the mother of memory.
2. *Attention:* Conscious attention helps students to understand the importance of the subject and learning can be acquired much easily. Subconscious attention indicates physical presence but you could very well be mentally absent. The details are stored in the subconscious mind and can be recollected later.
3. *Capacity:* The amount of information stored in the memory is unlimited. Let us check the capacity of the brain. Let us compare our brain to the Internet. For example, take a glass of water. Put a piece of chalk into it. It gets dissolved in the course of time. Though it is not visible, its impact is there. Same is the case with all our experiences.
4. *Experiences:* The more the experience, the more are the patterns created and based on the pattern we react or respond to. The patterns are so strongly imbibed that a small change resists the way we process any new information.

5. *Practice:* The more you practise the same thing, the more you become confident and it helps you to gain enough knowledge and learnings from what you have learned.

3.4: Boost Your Brain Power

We need to know and learn how to utilize the powers of our brain and mind. Science has advanced exponentially and a lot of research has been done on how to use it effectively and efficiently to improvise on our day to day activities. We have limitless mind and brain powers. During a television interview, Albert Einstein, one of the most brilliant minds, jokingly claimed that he utilizes only around 10 per cent of his mind. You have to constantly and consciously enhance the amount of brain power that you use. A balanced diet, rich in vitamins, Omega 3 helps to maintain a healthy brain.

3.5: Why Do We Forget?

The neurons in the brain capture information and connect with other cells (neurons) so that we are able to store and recall that particular information when it is needed. The connections are made through the synapse. Now, let us understand the different reasons why we forget in spite of the connections and associations.

1. *Interference:* While learning a new thing, old information interferes with new information and some are not able to manage and differentiate between the new and old, leading to differences in communication.
2. *Poor Attention:* Attention is the most valuable resource that we need to possess. Learning starts with alertness. During a session or a workshop, if the mind and brain are not active, it leads to poor attention span; hence, the information is not processed properly. Attention is to the mind what focussing

How to Develop Good Memory

the lens is to a camera.
3. *Less Interest:* Interest is the mother of memory and if there is low interest in the topic, there are breaks in the information flow. Important and related information is lost in the process.
4. *No Repetition:* Information that is learnt properly stays for a short period of time. One needs to repeat the information again and again over a period of time so that the connections are built strongly.
5. *Repression:* It is the unconscious forgetting of painful memories that is known as 'repression'. For example, forgetting unpleasant memories associated with your emotions of the past. Pleasant experiences are recalled more easily than unpleasant ones.
6. *Drugs:* Drugs affect the health of the brain, causing giddiness, stress, pain, uneasiness, loss of understanding and recall. Drugs are not just harmful to our brain but also damage the cells carrying important and useful information.
7. *Emotions:* Emotions play an important role in learning, understanding and recalling events. Positive and pleasant emotions help to recall better while unpleasant emotions loosen the connections between the neurons and widen the gap between the information flow. We use our mind to think and brain to take decisions. When they are not aligned with each other, we find it difficult to take decisions.

3.6: Ingredients for Powerful Memory

1. *Concentration:* Proper concentration leads to proper understanding, evaluation, remembering and recalling. The complete flow is disturbed if concentration is not in place. Our brains have not been developed for multitasking. Concentration calls for doing one activity at a time so that complete attention can be provided and the ultimate result

can be achieved. Multitasking disturbs the flow of information flowing in one direction and diverts the energy in multiple directions resulting in defocus and ultimately, incomplete work.

2. While studying, a student should only deal with the subject he is learning at the moment. All the other books should be placed away, so that he or she does not get distracted.

3. *Clear Thinking:* A well-articulated schedule can help you plan and manage what needs to be accomplished. Clear thinking helps to manage your daily schedules and get things done. Thinking is also a process and one needs to learn how to think. There are several styles of thinking—lateral thinking, divergent thinking, creative thinking, planned thinking, etc. Based on the use and need, one can think and go ahead with execution.

4. *Environment:* Learning requires an environment and that's the reason it is taught in the closed classroom, with seating arrangements made in such a way that each student faces the trainer/teacher and learns from him/her. An environment of learning is created and the subjects are managed in that limited time frame. For debates or discussions, a round-table structure is suggested so that each student can see the other and understand his/her viewpoint.

5. *Habits:* Certain good habits and behaviour patterns make or break a student's learning patterns. Regularly taking the same place at a stipulated time can create a learning pattern in one's brain. Good habits can be an encouragement and it will play as a motivating factor for the brain in the learning process.

6. Once developed, it's difficult to break, as the brain designs a roadmap for your success. Habits follow with to-do list, activities, proper food, sleep and play timings.

7. *Interest:* Interest holds the information consciously as well as at a subconscious level. We all love to play, listen to stories, watch a movie or just relax with soothing music around.
8. Finding our core interest helps us activate our cells and put them to active work. Our neurons are ready to take in information and act as per the directions. You can be either a slave or a master of your mind. Once the interest is generated, it becomes easy for you to mould it the way you wish because it helps to identify the core values that you carry ahead.
9. *Relaxation:* Relaxation of mind and body leads to proper concentration, provides energy and results in a sound mind and brain to take proper decisions related to studies, play or revision. Concentration occurs most naturally when body and mind are relaxed. After a few minutes or hours, sit down in a relaxed posture and leave all your controls and make your body light. Don't stress yourself or be rigid. This position helps to maintain the body temperature and adjust with the environment, which makes your body feel better. During this period, the organs get more energized to support your system to run efficiently and become more productive.
10. *Repetition:* Brain captures the information and connects with related topics for future use. Information can be held for a few minutes since we all have been blessed with short term remembrance, as we capture a lot of information and learnings throughout the day. Repetition strengthens the connections and helps us store information for a longer period. More practice/more revisions helps students to recall information during the exam period.

3.7: Tips to Improve Your Brainpower

1. Develop a habit of positive thinking.

2. Practise concentration after every short interval.
3. Practise creative skills to improve visualization.
4. Imagination improves the power of the mind.
5. Observe brain rhythms—take a 20-minute break for every 90–120 minutes of mental work.
6. Be aware of what is happening around you while you are studying topics that are interesting or not as interesting. Change the timings, if required.
7. Physical exercise, particularly yogic asanas, is vital for brainpower development.
8. Spend time in open spaces and with nature; it refreshes the mind and also stimulates the processes of the mind.
9. Take proper care of your diet and eat at regular intervals.
10. Observe your sleep cycle and relax your mind and body when the need arises.

3.8: Summary

Summarize what you have understood from this chapter—your takeaways—and how you would use it daily.

Chapter 4

Learning Style

4.1: Introduction

Learning is a process. Is there a way of learning which fits everyone? We all learn with a certain goal in mind—be it grasping information, feeding knowledge to the brain, clearing exams, understanding concepts or just to pass time.

We need to know what suits us and what we benefit from the most.

4.2: Identify Your Learning Style

Aim: To know your learning style for better performance.

Learning objective: Understand methods and systems that need to be adopted for better learning and performance style.

What you need: A questionnaire and a ball pen

What to do: Read the questions, understand and attempt them.

		A	B	C
1	While learning a new game, I prefer to	read the instructions.	listen or ask.	learn by 'trial and error'.
2	While travelling to a new place, I	follow a map.	ask for directions.	follow a compass.

3	While ordering a new dish, I		follow the menu.		call a waiter to explain.		guess how the food would taste.
4	To teach someone something, I		write or draw instructions.		explain verbally.		demonstrate.
5	I tend to say:		'I see what you mean.'		'I hear what you say.'		'I know how you feel.'
6	I tend to say:		'show me.'		'tell me.'		'let me do it.'
7	I tend to say:		'watch how I do it.'		'listen to me explain.'		'do it with me.'
8	I prefer these leisure activities:		visiting places such as museums or galleries.		listen to/play musical instruments, sing/attend concerts.		play a game/engage in physical activities.
9	While shopping, I generally		look and decide.		discuss with the store staff.		learn by 'trial and error.'
10	While learning a new skill, I		watch and perform.		hear, understand and then do it.		learn by 'trial and error.'
11	While choosing from a restaurant's menu, I		imagine what the food will look like.		talk through the options in my head.		imagine what the food would taste and feel like.
12	While listening to a band, I		visualize a song or its lyrics.		engage with the lyrics and the rhythm of the song.		get connected to the feel and sway.

13	While concentrating on a subject, I	consciously create images.	listen patiently.	focus on the activity.
14	I remember things best by	visualizing and pictorial representation.	repeating words and key points aloud.	counting your body parts.
15	My first memory is of	images like places, objects and persons.	sounds like instruments, songs, rhymes and dialogues.	activities like touching, feeling or tasting.
16	When I am anxious, I	visualize the worst-case scenarios.	keep on talking.	fiddle.
17	I feel especially connected to others because of	how they look.	what they tell me.	how they make me feel.
18	When I revise for an exam, I	take notes by using colours.	read aloud.	use gestures.
19	While explaining something to someone, I tend to	draw or visualize what I mean.	explain verbally.	teach by 'trial and error.'
20	Most of my free time is spent in	engaging in visual medium—watching TV, nature and thinking.	listening to music, songs and drama.	activities like playing indoor or outdoor games.

Let us analyse how you have done.

4.2.1: Explanation

If you have chosen your answers in column 'A', you are more inclined towards following a list of words that shows signs of Visual Learners, i.e., the type of learners who are more prone to using words, both in speech and writing and visualizing. They are those who *read, look, follow, see, show, watch, imagine, visualize, visit, engage and draw*.

If you have chosen your answers from column 'B', you are more inclined towards following a list of words that shows signs of Auditory Learners, i.e., the type of learners who prefer sound and music. They are those who *listen, ask, call, explain, hear, tell, talk and discuss*.

If you have chosen your answers from column 'C', you are more inclined towards following a list of words that shows signs of Kinaesthetic Learners, i.e., the type of learners who prefer using body, hands and the sense of touch. They are those who *follow, feel, demonstrate, experiment* and *teach*.

Count and write how many times you have marked your answers in columns A, B and C. Note them down in the box given below:

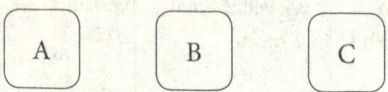

Now we are going to explore the prominent qualities seen in visual, auditory and kinaesthetic learners, along with certain tips for improving each learning style. We are also going to assess the areas where they can do well and those where they falter.

4.3: Visual Learners

A visual learner is one who adopts a learning style in which he or she utilizes graphs, charts, maps and diagrams. A visual learner memorizes information mostly in terms of images, pictures and symbols. It is one of the three basic types of learning styles in the Fleming VAK/VARK model.

4.3.1: Qualities of visual learners:

- Learn best by seeing, visualizing, etc.
- Visualize what they think
- Imagine consequences much in advance
- Enjoy relating to colours
- Notice colourful dynamic visual effects in movies
- Easily relate to movies with their stories
- Enjoy watching 2D and 3D formats
- Follow written instructions easily
- Think most of the time
- Daydreamers
- Good at reading and vocabulary
- Remember faces easily

4.3.2: Visual learners excel in:

- Pictorial representation
- Reading and visualizing maps
- Creating an outline of a text
- Designing a concept visually
- Understanding and representing
- Verbal communication
- Creating a big picture/vision
- Brain mapping
- Artistic activities
- Using image editing tools
- Solving jigsaw puzzles and the Rubik's Cube

4.3.3: Visual learners fail in:

- Verbal communication
- Creating ideas, if concepts are not clear
- Communicating and responding with other types of learners, especially auditory learners
- Logical thinking
- Activity-based learning
- Deciphering colour
- Focussing

4.3.4: Important tips

- Use visualization to recall points
- Provide clear written instructions or communication and they follow correctly
- Prefer one-on-one interaction
- Learn easily with creative, story-style or splash maps
- Ensure that notes, written on the board, are clearly visible
- Convert a monotonous texts or passages into pictures (brain mapping—taught in next lessons)
- Use colourful and agile methods to write notes rather than monochromatic and linear ones
- Sit at a place where he or she can look around, observe facial expressions of people and their body language
- Avoid activities that rely on rote memorization

4.3.5: Remedies

Research indicates that visual cues such as symbols, signs, alphabets and algorithms help us improve our retrieving and remembering skills.

Let us explore some remedies helpful to visual learners to excel.

4.3.6: Activity: Draw an image

Close your eyes for a minute. Think about anything that you have interest in and run it like a movie or with animated effects in your mind. Open your eyes and draw a picture of what you had just visualized.

4.3.7: Activity: Visual interpretation

Draw pictures for the following words mentioned in each box.

Speaker	Save water	Fire	Peace	Love	Happy
Road	Danger	Connect	Live	Education	Dead end
Smile	Angry	Music	Dance	School	Winner

4.4: Auditory Learners

An auditory learner is one who learns through better communication, listening and speech recognition. They recognize a sound, decode it and understand it better.

4.4.1: Qualities of auditory learners

- Learn best by listening
- Like to read aloud and learn better with repetitions
- Good at explaining the concepts, directions, etc.

- Mostly speak aloud
- Learn better in class if they concentrate and listen to the sessions
- Enjoy activities related to sound, e.g., music, concerts, etc.
- Follow spoken directions easily
- Good speakers
- Easily remember names
- Notice sound effects in movies

4.4.2: Auditory learners excel in:

- Listening to lectures consciously
- Writing responses
- Taking oral examinations
- Speech recognition
- Having telephonic conversations
- Addressing an audience
- Listening to rhymes
- Understanding numbers conveyed to them verbally
- Understanding directions given verbally

4.4.3: Auditory learners fail in:

- Completing exams in a given time
- Imagination and visualization skills
- Understanding written directions
- Understanding symbols, icons, drawings, etc.
- Concrete thinking
- Brain mapping
- Mingling with a mixed crowd
- Multitasking
- Taking dictations

4.4.4: Important tips

- Use word association to remember facts and points
- Give oral, along with written, instructions
- Watch audio-visuals to complement the written test
- Repeat loudly and record sounds for future reference
- Listen to music while studying which helps relieve stress
- Record study material and listen to it frequently
- Participate in group discussions

4.4.5: Remedies

- Read aloud
- Go to concerts or musical nights
- Listen to his or her own musical collection regularly
- Read poetry aloud
- Spend one hour to listen to unfamiliar styles of music
- Play the keyboard and learn simple melodies
- Learn to identify birds by the sounds they make
- Listen in silence and identify the source of the sound
- Sing while taking a shower
- Learn to write and recite poetry or join any group

4.4.6: Activity: Different sounds

Sit in a calm place. Keep a notebook handy and time your watch to two minutes. Close your eyes and consciously observe the sounds you hear. Note down at least five different sounds:

1) _____
2) _____
3) _____
4) _____
5) _____

4.4.7: Activity: Intensity of sound

Classify the sounds below in terms of intensity on a scale of 1 to 10, with 1 being the lowest and 10 the highest.

Column A consists of personal experiences based on the sound you hear at your place or at work every day.

Column B consists of the intensity of the sound in silence that you can hear.

Let's imagine a scenario—movie theatre.

Column A: You may not be aware of the high frequency of the sound since you are engrossed in the movie or you may get disturbed.

Column B: Record the actual intensity of the sound if someone breaks a glass in the movie theatre.

Create your own scenario and fill in the table below:

(Scenario) _____

Activity	A	B
Breaking of a glass		
Birds chirping		
Rotating ceiling fan		
A mixer grinder being turned on		
Door bell		
A motorbike accelerating		
A cellphone ringing		
A knock at the door		
A musical instrument (guitar) playing		
Vehicles moving in heavy traffic		

Tip: Logical thinking and experiential thinking may differ based on actual, i.e., present vs past, experience.

4.5: Kinaesthetic Learners

A kinaesthetic learner, or tactile learner, is one who deals with learning through physical activities, touch, feel and action. Trial and error is the most prominent since the learner likes to explore more rather than use the traditional methods of learning.

4.5.1: Qualities of kinaesthetic learners:

- Learn best by performing activities
- Mostly read while walking and moving around
- Respond well when they are involved
- Mostly good at outdoor sports
- Enjoy dancing or watching action in movies
- Enact what they are reading
- Enjoy adventurous trips
- Like mechanical work
- Cannot sit idle for a long time

4.5.2: Kinaesthetic learners excel in:

- Short answers
- Multiple choice questions
- Match the columns
- Fill in the blanks
- Action-oriented tasks
- Outdoor and indoor activities
- Sports
- Activities involving body movements such as dancing, etc.
- Speeches

4.5.3: Kinaesthetic learners fail in:

- Lengthy tests
- Writing long essays

- Writing long descriptions
- Rote learning
- Listening
- Creativity
- Spatial skills
- Mathematical formulae
- Recalling numbers

4.5.4: Important tips

- Use a practical approach for learning
- Learn effectively through different role-plays or activities
- Prefer short sessions rather than long ones
- Learn better using flash cards
- Walk or enact while reading or studying
- Listen to short stories to understand concepts
- Sit where his or her movements are not restricted
- Illustrate ideas by drawing maps, graphs, tables, etc.

4.5.5: Remedies

- Join any outdoor sports
- Learn to juggle
- Learn activities like martial arts
- Exercise regularly
- Learn crafts, such as origami, clay modelling, charades, etc., where the use of hands is more significant and involves helping others
- Develop hand-eye coordination by tossing, basketball, etc.
- Play video games that require quick reflexes
- Take formal lessons in dancing, sports, aerobics, etc.

4.5.6: Activity: Blindfold

Blindfold yourself and move around your house to explore something new.

Note down what you have touched and felt without taking off the blindfold. Now take it off and note down the objects you are able to recall from your memory.

Soft:	Slimy:	Textured:
Smooth:	Rough:	Plain:
Vibrating:	Hot:	Cold:

4.5.6.1 Assessment

Using the VAK activities, observation and analysis, rate your overall learning skill. (Grade yourself from 0 to 10, with 0 being the lowest and 10 being the highest.)

Date: _____

Style		Reading	Writing	Listening	Understanding
K					
V					
A					

After two months, you need to take the test again and compare the results.

4.6: Action Plan

- Adopt your learning style and improvise for better performance.
- Use your non-dominant hand to do regular daily rituals like brushing, holding, writing, etc.
- Schedule yourself, in either the morning or evening, to observe your surroundings.

- Discuss a topic with your friends, family members and check your knowledge.
- Pay attention to small things and help others if they are looking for or have misplaced anything.
- Study using your own style and note down the changes after improvising.
- Record your activities daily and maintain your diary.

4.7: Summary

Summarize what you have understood from this chapter—your takeaways—and how you would use it daily.

Chapter 5

Right and Left Brain

5.1: Introduction

Our brain comprises neuron and neural networks connecting other neurons to store information. Researchers are still trying to identify activities handled by the right and the left side of the brain. Humans coordinate and communicate using both sides. Let us now find out how they work.

5.2: Left Brain

- Believed to be more logical, linear and realistic
- Practical and helps you understand the concepts as shown in front of you
- Result-oriented
- Structured and conscious mode of thinking
- Experienced and experimental
- Focussed on systematic representation
- Solves mathematical expressions in a structured way and is process-oriented
- Detail-oriented and analyses the situation based on the current scenario, experience and results evolved in the past
- Can think only within certain boundaries and are target-oriented

People have either a dominant left or right brain. Let us analyse if a person is left-brained with the following activity.

5.2.1: Activity: Left brain

Aim: To analyse and see how your left brain functions.

Learning objective: To analyse how much you know about the left side of your brain.

What you need: A book, a pen, a pencil, an eraser and crayons.

What to do: Read the information carefully. Analyse what you have understood and note it below.

Tip: The right side of the brain uses the information gathered by the left side of the brain.

5.3: Right Brain

- Believed to be creative and imaginative
- Identifies colours, music and art
- Visualizes dreams, aspirations, etc., clearly
- Explores beyond by not restricting to time, place, shapes, etc.
- Processes emotions, sympathy, empathy and feelings
- Intuitive
- Thinks outside the box, can be illogical too

5.3.1: Activity: Right brain

Aim: To help you analyse and see how your right brain functions.

Learning objective: To analyse how much you know about the right side of the brain.

What you need: A book, a pen, a pencil, an eraser and crayons.

What to do: Read the information carefully. Visualize and draw; you can also use symbols. Note it down below.

Tip: While you are reading, understand the concepts, symbolize and try to create weird or unusual images in your mind. Increase or decrease the size of the image, add colours, connect them with unusual objects, etc.

Now complete the checklist below to analyse whether you are left-brain oriented or right-brain oriented.

5.4: Checklist (tick whichever is applicable)

1. Able to understand concepts
2. Able to read words properly
3. Able to picturize the meaning
4. Able to learn properly and reproduce on repetition
5. Can visualize what has been read
6. Can feel what has been read
7. Can decide on your own after understanding a concept
8. Can recall in the same sequence with repetition
9. Cannot recall words in spite of repetition
10. Can connect with music, art or drawing easily

If you have checked items 1, 2, 4 and 8, you have used the left side of the brain.

If you have checked items 3, 5, 6, 7, 9 and 10, you have used the right side of the brain.

5.5: How to Improve the LEFT Side of the Brain

- Analyse the problem and come up with probable solutions based on your experience, learnings, etc.
- Learn a new computer programming language and understand the logic.
- Set a goal—short-term, mid-term and long-term.
- Prepare your own time log and try to stick to it.
- Organize your filling system or desk.
- Prepare a to-do list and tick off the items you have completed.
- Plan a project. Break it down into small tasks and schedule

a timeline for each of them.
- Discipline yourself to be on time for appointments.
- Write down about any activity or task in hand in the most detailed manner possible.
- Use logic, probabilities and data during a decision-making process.
- Play logic games—Sudoku, math puzzles, quizzes on analytical reasoning, etc. Use logic to assemble a model kit by following the instructions provided.
- Note down daily expenses every day in a notebook.
- Prepare a list of all items and tick them off when purchased.
- Organize books, files, audio tapes, medicines at home as per their categories.
- Prepare a family tree.
- Observe closely and find out errors in your bank passbooks, hotel bills, electricity bills, phone bills, etc.
- Keep things neat and tidy in their proper places.
- Note down and keep a reminder for expiry dates, due dates, policies, driving license, insurance, etc.
- Use a dictionary to find out meanings of commonly used words and use them when you talk.

5.5.1: Activity: How to study

Problem: How should I study to get better results?

Activate your *left* brain cells and write the points down in the space below:

Solutions:
_____
_____

5.5.2: Activity: Short-, mid- and long-term goals

Short-term goal (a day, a week or a month): _____
Mid-term goal (3–6 months): _____
Long-term goal (1 year, 3 years or 5 years): _____

5.5.3: Activity: Time log

Time logs help channelize your thinking about the time to be allotted for study, play, rest, leisure, etc. When you are admitted to school, it provides you with a timetable about the subjects to be taught and when and by whom, so that you are aware of the subjects being taught at a particular time and the duration of every class.

Let us create a weekly plan that will enable us to know the activity to be performed at a particular time.

Timing	Monday	Tuesday	Wednesday	Thursday	Friday	Saturday	Sunday
4:00							
5:00							
6:00							
7:00							
8:00							
9:00							
10:00							
11:00							
12:00							
13:00							
14:00							
15:00							
16:00							
17:00							
18:00							

19:00						
20:00						
21:00						
22:00						
23:00						
24:00						

5.5.4: Activity: To-do list

Planning is the first step towards completing any activity. As a student, a lot of activities such as studying, school assignments, tuition, homework and surprise tests, and creative activities, such as drawing, craft, art book, need to be performed. If planned in a proper way, you will be able to prioritize your work. Once the urgent and lesser important tasks are completed, you will be able to work on the remaining important work.

Let us plan our day based on the above pointers:

Date: _____

After the completion of the task, you can tick the box provided next to the activity.

	Urgent		Important		Later
	Needs immediate attention		Should be completed as soon as possible		Needs to be completed
☐		☐		☐	
☐		☐		☐	
☐		☐		☐	
☐		☐		☐	
☐		☐		☐	
☐		☐		☐	
☐		☐		☐	
☐		☐		☐	

☐		☐		☐	
☐		☐		☐	
☐		☐		☐	
☐		☐		☐	
☐		☐		☐	
☐		☐		☐	

5.5.5: Activity: Plan a project

Project Name (For example, a science project):

Material	Quantity	Responsibility	Timeline
Cardboard paper	5	<Names of those responsible>	<Date> <Time>

5.5.6: Activity: Test of numerical ability

Try to recall the following numbers below:

4	7	9	0	3	6	2	6	8	3	5	2	7	3	5	9	0	1

Answer Sheet:

5.5.7: Activity: Reminder note

Instrument	Details	Last date	Account	Remarks
Driving License	no.abc123	31.12.2018	Personal	Paid at RTO

5.6: How to Improve the Functioning of the Right Brain

1. Pen down your ideas in an **idea book** and keep it handy.
2. Draw or stick pictures about what you wish to become in future. For example, a wish list of trips you want to take or things you wish to have.
3. Redecorate your home. Add toys, posters, etc.
4. Develop a concept and design your own logo.
5. Gather your friends around and start a brainstorming session on an important issue.
6. Conceptualize a new product.
7. Smile and make others smile too; it will usher in positivity.
8. Enjoy the smallest moment in your life.

9. Help and support your friends whenever they need you.
10. Listen to music and go for concerts.
11. Meet a new person every day.
12. Observe carefully and consciously to find out a new aspect of anything, which you did not know earlier.
13. Discuss the pros and cons of any situation with your team.
14. Convert alphabets into pictures. Draw alphabets only through pictures.
15. Indulge in activities such as learning new recipes, origami and Best-Out-of-Waste crafts, etc.
16. Learn to fly a kite and enjoy.
17. Drive or walk to 'nowhere'.
18. Go for a run every day or participate in a marathon.
19. Go to any historic place or to gardens, etc., and click photographs.
20. Simply dance!
21. Sit at a quiet place and daydream.
22. Engage with children and turn into a child.
23. Cry if it makes you feel better.
24. Enjoy nature. Write down details of what you see, observe, feel or smell.
25. Participate in spiritual sessions.
26. Express your feelings.
27. Ask for help and counsel.
28. Go on excursions with your friends or family members.
29. Spend a full day with yourself without a plan.
30. Give surprises! Plan a surprise visit to your family member or friend without informing them.
31. Taste different food, enjoy and appreciate the taste.
32. Learn different activities.
33. Learn a new language.
34. Get involved in activities; don't analyse. Don't give your views.

5.6.1: Activity: Improve vocabulary

Vocabulary needs to be added every day. The question is—how can we recall what we have learnt? The easiest way is to link, associate, create a vivid story taking the word and connecting with the meaning in a way that activates the creative side of the brain.

Word	Meaning	Create Story

5.6.2 : Activity: Prepare a family tree

5.7: Summary

Summarize what you have understood from this chapter—your takeaways—and how you would use it daily.

Chapter 6

Brain-Mind-Memory

6.1: Introduction

In this chapter, we will try to understand the relationship between the brain, mind and memory, and how they work in synchronization. They are interconnected and bind together to form wilful thinking rather than wishful thinking. Our brain directs the mind and the information is transmitted for further execution. On execution, the experiences are stored in the subconscious mind, i.e., the warehouse, for future use or just for study and ready reference.

6.2: Learning Objective

- Messages are transmitted in the form of thoughts that take the form of language, and are translated into words, signs or symbols. They form a meaningful message, and then, it is conceived by the mind. The mind passes the message to the brain and provides direction to act, hold or lose the information. The brain acts on the message and is passed to the respective part of the body, for example, a student's name is called during attendance and he or she raises the hand, denoting his or her presence. The motor skills and this communication are stored in the memory, which then create a pattern and it is stored for future use.
- Reactions are communicated and segregated as good, bad

or neutral. Incidents are stored in the form of memory in different parts of the brain.
- The more you learn, your capacity to learn becomes greater. The more you acquire information and send it to the memory, it has the capability to hold the information, place it in the space within, and make it powerful. The ultimate creative capacity of the brain, for all practical purposes, is infinite.
- Creative thinking can generate ideas; hence, have a richer and denser network, with a greater number of interconnections between neurons that accommodate a wider range of ideas, feelings, emotions, intuitions, etc.

6.3: Brain Response

The brain scans and interprets information as reliable or unreliable. Based on the flow of information to the brain, it decides to *freeze*, *fight* the situation or *flee* from it.

For example: If you notice an angry and hysterical person coming towards you, you will need to decide, based on the reasoning, analysis and other factors, whether to *fight* him or her, *freeze* and gauge the situation, or *flee* from it. During this situation, certain parts of the brain release neurochemicals that affect the body and mobilizes its energies towards fighting or fleeing.

Our brain's primary function is to **protect** us from harm and ensure that every part in our body is working.

It is **responsible** for maintaining the entire functioning of our body.

Its **capacity** for receiving, storing and acting on information is not complete unless it coordinates with all other systems in our body.

All our **life-support** systems are closely linked, and dependent on each other. For example, we would not be able to digest food without a **circulatory system** that enables us to absorb and supply nutrients to all parts of the body.

The **brain** ensures that all these actions take place at just the right time.

The **sensory organs**—eyes, ears, nose, tongue and skin— help protect our body. The human sense organs contain receptors that relay information through sensory neurons to the appropriate places within the nervous system.

The internal receptors gather information related to things like temperature, touch and body position.

Our brain is more than just an ultra-sophisticated computer, the hub of a complex communications system.

If it were not so, human beings would have been like robots that, when programmed to behave in a particular way, would have no choice but to react to a given circumstance in a predetermined fashion.

The brain makes you an **individual**—unique and distinct from everybody else.

It is not just **responsible** for coordinating and controlling all the activities.

Our brain enables us to perform these **functions**:

- Using language
- Planning and assessing
- Reasoning and learning
- Feeling and being more creative
- Appreciating creativity in others

Scientists and researchers suspect that everything that goes on in our brain, even the smallest information such as the preference to a kind of music over another, may well turn out to be the result of specific electro-chemical events that happen within.

6.4: Neurons

A neuron is a specialized cell that receives, processes and transmits information to different parts of the brain in the form of chemical (feelings) or electrical (words) signals. It consists of dendrites and axons that are primarily agents to receive and share information with other neurons.

Nerve fibres within the brain are responsible for sending stimuli (messages) to the cell body, passing them to other neurons, or taking them away from the cell body.

6.5: Types of Neurons

Neurons are of three basic types:

Sensory neurons bring in the stimulus from a sense organ or internal receptor.

Connector (or association) neurons sort information in our brain.

The **spinal cord** and **motor neurons** relay messages back to our body and initiate some kind of action.

6.6: Brain Regions

Every part of the brain performs certain functions. For example,

- The Cerebellum is responsible for coordination.
- The Hippocampus is responsible for storing memories.
- Nerve cells (neurons) communicate within the brain.
- Information is passed on from one area of the brain to other areas through the most complex network of interconnected neurons. Information, via electrical impulses, transmitted from one neuron to many others is done through a process called 'neurotransmission'.

There are three major divisions of the brain, each with a specific purpose. The major divisions of the brain are forebrain, midbrain and hindbrain.

6.7: Forebrain

The forebrain is the largest part of the brain. It includes the cerebral hemispheres, the thalamus and the hypothalamus.

6.7.1: Function of forebrain

- Chewing
- Movement of eyeballs
- Vision
- Sensations
- Hearing
- Phonation
- Intelligence
- Memorizing
- Personality
- Respiration
- Salivation
- Swallowing

6.8: Midbrain

The midbrain and the hindbrain together make up the brainstem. The midbrain is the portion of the brainstem that connects the hindbrain and the forebrain.

6.8.1: Function of midbrain

- Auditory
- Visual responses
- Motor skills

6.9: Hindbrain

The hindbrain starts at the tip of the spinal cord.

6.9.1 Functions of hindbrain

- Breathing
- Maintaining heart rate
- Digestion
- Maintaining balance and equilibrium
- Movements and coordination
- Conduction of sensory information

6.10: Working with Minds

Our mind is an imaginary and perceptual tool with multiple faculties, including conscious thinking, perception, assessment, memory and facilitating as a dictionary. It holds the superpowers of visualization and imagination. What you can hold in your mind can be perceived and made possible if you have strong faith, hope and patience to transform it into reality. It can also process feelings and emotions resulting in actions (good or bad). Our mind is a support mechanism for what you believe is true and stores that information.

There are different kinds of minds. Let us explore them one by one with examples.

6.10.1: Executive mind

An executive mind helps to analyse a situation, considers different perspectives based on available information, feelings, relationship, takes accountability to provide solutions, orders and takes the situation in control.

6.10.1.1: Skills

Coordination, decision-making, assessment, giving orders, controlling, enforcing, making rules and setting priorities.

_____

_____

6.10.2.2: Activity: Exams

Assume that your exams begin in two days and you need to complete your assignments, attend a wedding ceremony and revise five chapters out of eight. You also have to read three chapters afresh and then revise them too.

How do you think your executive mind would handle such a situation? Apply your executive mind and note down your views below.

_____

_____

6.10.3: Wondering mind

A wondering mind is more like a kite which is drifting away. It flies, floats and moves like a free bird in the sky. It is not bound by any force.

6.10.3.1: Skills

- Exploring
- Learning
- Creating
- Discovering
- Inferring
- Experimenting
- Intuitive
- Relying on other parts of the mind for input, usually on the executive mind for permission

6.10.3.2: Activity: Classroom

You are sitting in a classroom and your teacher is teaching a subject. You are physically present but not attentive towards the session. Your wondering mind has taken over and now you are within your own self. Write down all the places you can visit:

_____
_____
_____

6.10.4: Organizing mind

An organizing mind decides the manner in which any activity or project needs to be done. It analyses a situation internally and visualizes it in the mind, helping the executive mind to perform the action.

6.10.4.1: Skills

- Analysing
- Sorting
- Crafting
- Ordering
- Sequencing
- Rationalizing
- Comparing
- Acting on rules that have been established through past experiences

6.10.4.2: Activity: Event

You have been appointed to arrange a trip to Esselworld, Mumbai, by your teacher. Use your organizing skills and note down how you are going to organize this event.

6.10.5: Reacting mind

A reacting mind relies on a situation-based thinking and is dependent on many factors. It acts based on experience, the information in hand, thought process, who it is dealing with—the emotionally strong, emotionally weak, physically strong or physically weak. The reaction differs for every situation. It can differ from person to person too.

6.10.5.1: Skills

A reacting mind interprets emotions such as:

- Anger
- Fear
- Sorrow
- Joy
- Boredom
- Embarrassment
- Humour
- Love
- Compassion
- Psychic pain
- Pleasure

6.10.5.2: Activity: React

Assume that an angry crowd is coming towards you. React in one of the following situations given below.

Situation 1: You are tough and can handle the situation.

Situation 2: You are fearful.

Situation 3: You know that you have taken the right decision.

6.10.6: Knowing mind

Based on the information in hand—the experiences gained and regular updates—the knowing mind gathers information and passes it on to the other parts of the body for processing. It captures the information and helps other minds to decide, analyse or take action.

6.10.6.1: Skills

- Sees
- Hears
- Smells
- Taste
- Possesses tactile and kinaesthetic experience
- Collects information and presents it to the other minds for processing

6.10.6.2: Activity: Senses

Close your eyes and visualize a day in your classroom. Note down incidents that take place.

When you are at a party, try to name the dishes without looking at the tags on them.

6.10.7: The silent mind

A quiet mind, but active enough to think beyond. Our silent mind is independent, not dependent on other minds for views, analysis or judgement. It thinks in its own sphere and is more observant than judgmental. It performs activities related to our body.

6.10.7.1: Skills

- Controlling our bodily functions
- Breathing
- Digesting
- Creating
- Immunity
- Eliminating
- Thirst
- Hunger
- Body temperature
- Regulating weight
- Growth

6.10.7.2: Activity: Observation

Make a note of your breathing carefully and as you observe, note down your feelings, emotions, state of mind, etc., below:

_____
_____
_____

6.11: Memory is the Function of All Five Minds

Our memory can be compared to a library or a records-storage room of a large corporation.

It records selected information from all parts of the mind, stores it and later returns it, not always efficiently or productively and not always when needed or requested.

Follow these four rules to cleanse your inner being:

- Say what you mean. Mean what you say.
- Don't say it to anyone unless you can say it to everyone.
- Don't keep inside what you cannot say aloud.
- Don't say it unless it is true, useful or kind.

6.11.1: Activity: Source and solutions

Here are some obstacles we all face in our day-to-day lives. After learning about the five minds, what, according to you, is the possible source of the mental block, or in other words, which mind is responsible for a certain kind of obstacle? Finally, which mind takes the final call towards a possible solution? Analyse the blocks carefully and fill in the blanks.

Block	Possible Source	Possible Solution
I am terrified of speaking in public. I get tongue-tied and break sweat.		
I forget people's names in important situations.		
When I sit for my exams, my mind turns to mush. I panic and cannot add five and eight.		

6.11.2: Activity: Executive decisions

Two or more parts of the minds are in conflict and an executive decision requires to be taken.

Which parts of the mind do you think are disagreeing in the following situation?

1. I have trouble setting goals—analytical and emotional

2. I cannot make up my mind about/studying a particular subject/starting something new/taking a decision—analytical and emotional

3. I am often too shy at discussions/parties—noticing others and knowing oneself

4. I should quit smoking but I just cannot—immediate physical pleasure and decision for long-term good

5. Learning new things is difficult for me—natural curiosity and negative skill evaluation

6. Stress gives me headache/heartburn/hives—emotions and immune system

6.11.3: Activity: Mission or goal or both

Explore the difference between mission and goal

- Earn a law degree
- Be a good friend, develop a joyful relationship
- Make your community a better place
- Cook dinner
- Complete the assignment on time
- Raise funds for your school
- Help others
- Target your income for the next one year
- Provide security for an unknown person

6.12: Summary

Summarize what you have understood from this chapter—your takeaway—and how you would use it daily.

Chapter 7

United Method

7.1: Introduction

Alphabets form words, words form images and images create stories. Our brain is tuned to think about different ideas at any given time. Then, we set our own rules and try to change or convert ideas into a meaningful picture. The united method helps connect words, sentences, symbols, images and helps build confidence.

7.2: Activity: Test Your Memory

Aim: To help you understand the difference between trained and untrained memory.

Learning objective: To know how our brain and capability to recall works.

What you need: Exercise sheet (provided on the next page), a pen and a writing pad

What to do: Just take a moment to indicate if you would like to improve in each of the following areas, and we shall provide you the right tools, systems and techniques to do so. Tick wherever applicable.

1. A sheet with forty words that you need to memorize has been provided.
2. There are four columns with ten words in each.
3. Each word, in a sequence, carries two marks and each

word, in no particular order, carries one mark.
4. There is no negative marking.
5. Let us begin.
6. Scores shall be calculated column wise. For example, in Column A, if you get all right in the sequence, you get 20 marks.

In Column B, if you get the first five in the sequence right, and others in no particular order right but related to that column, you get 10 + 5 = 15 marks.

In Column C, if you get the first five in a sequence right, with a gap of three words and then two words from the same column, you get 10 + 2 = 12 marks.

In Column D, if you get the first five answers right and later, words that are not in the list or jumbled words from other columns, you get no marks. Your score becomes 10. Now your overall score becomes 20 + 15 + 12 + 10 = 47.

7.2.1: Random words: Question sheet

S. No.	Column A	S. No	Column B	S. No	Column C	S. No	Column D
1	Parrot	11	Mango	21	Television	31	Knife
2	Car	12	Mobile	22	Stopwatch	32	Roll
3	Flowers	13	Box	23	Remote	33	Bullet
4	Diary	14	CD player	24	Mouse	34	Cupboard
5	Computer	15	Light	25	AC	35	Rambo
6	Chair	16	Policemen	26	Visiting card	36	Doraemon
7	T-shirt	17	School bus	27	Heater	37	India
8	Watch	18	Pen	28	London	38	Mickey
9	Speaker	19	Stationary	29	Radio	39	Pizza
10	Purse	20	Ruler	30	Presentation	40	Bag

Now cover the sheet and write the answers below.

7.2.2: Random Words: Answer sheet

S. No.	Column A	S. No.	Column B	S. No.	Column C	S. No.	Column D
1		11		21		31	
2		12		22		32	
3		13		23		33	
4		14		24		34	
5		15		25		35	
6		16		26		36	
7		17		27		37	
8		18		28		38	
9		19		29		39	
10		20		30		40	

Now, find the **Interpretation Sheet** below to access your views, feelings and observations during the Memory Test. This assessment sheet shall help you analyse the pitfalls, and it serves as a performance indicator, too. Please go through the document first and then start filling in the Assessment Sheet (Untrained column).

7.3: How to Interpret

Once you have memorized the random numbers, fill in the 'Untrained' column in the assessment sheet.

Explanation

Duration: Time provided to memorize the set of forty words.

Sequential: Write down the score of only those words that you have been able to memorize sequentially and columnwise. Count the scores and add them up. Mention the total score here:

Non-sequential: Write down the score of only those words that you have not been able to memorize sequentially. Count the scores and add them up. Mention the total score here.

Reverse: Write down the score of only those words that you have been able to memorize in the reverse order in a sequence. Count and mention the total score here:

Stress: During your studies or exams, are you stressed during or before the exam, even if you have learned the answer? Answer with 'yes', 'no', 'a little' or 'never'.

Conscious thinking: Did you associate and connect the words with a proper thinking process on how you can recall a set of forty words by using images, symbols, experience or any other form of association? Answer with 'Yes', 'no' or 'somewhat'.

Systems: Did you set up any rules for recall? Answer with 'Yes', 'no' or 'somewhat'.

Tools: Did you use any of the known tools used to recall long words, numbers, etc.? Answer with 'Yes', 'no' or 'somewhat'.

Process: Did you apply or form a stepwise process in recalling the words? Answer with 'Yes', 'no' or 'somewhat'.

Logical: Did you apply your logical brain, i.e. your left brain, since the instructions provided were to memorize in sequence? Answer with 'Yes', 'no' or 'somewhat'.

Creative ideas: Did you apply your creative brain, i.e. your right brain, for creative activities? Answer with 'Yes', 'no' or 'somewhat'.

Confidence: Were you confident about scoring high marks before you started memorizing? Answer with 'Yes', 'no' or 'somewhat'.

Fear: Were you afraid while memorizing—fear of failure, fear of forgetting, etc.? Answer with 'Yes', 'no' or 'somewhat'.

Results: After memorizing, were you confident of the results? Answer with 'Yes', 'no' or 'somewhat'.

Directions: Based on the result, one can decide upon the directions or field of interest based on the scores. Answer with 'Yes', 'No' or 'Somewhat'.

7.4: Assessment Sheet

Fill the 'untrained' column. Once you have learned the technique after going through the next few pages, fill in the 'trained' column and see the difference for yourself.

Parameters	Untrained	Trained
Duration	5 minutes	5 minutes
Sequence (in same order)		
Non-sequence		
Reverses (back to front)		
Stress		
Conscious thinking		
Systems		
Tools		
Process		
Logical		
Creative ideas		
Confidence		
Fear		
Results		
Directions		

Now, let us explore the technique as to how the neurons are connected and how they pass on the electrochemical signals from one neuron to another.

7.5: United Method

Aim: To help you to understand how your brain connects information and helps retrieve the same information accurately.

Learning objective: An effective use of the right and left brains in a synchronized way.

What you need: Complete attention and understanding of the Golden Rules.

Some students understand the concept and learn their lessons, some mug up while others just study for the sake of passing the examination. This increases the stress level as the date of the exam comes closer. Due to stress, a person may forget or go blank during the examination. Elders mug up the list of words or refer to the list to be followed.

7.5.1: Benefits

This technique will help:

- Reduce stress
- Form a process and recall with ease
- Memorize and recall whenever required
- Keep the information stored in either short- or long-term memory.

7.5.2: Usage

- To memorize long answers, paragraphs or points
- To learn with ease and make proper use of brain powers
- To understand the potential and effective use of the right and left brains.

7.5.3: Rules

The basic rules for things to be remembered are those that must fall into at least one of the following categories:

- Memorable
- Unique
- Recalled
- Chunked or linked

Rule No. 1, 2 and 3 are *mandatory*.

1. **Create a story**: Our brain loves stories as it provides us with logical thinking, imagination, visualization, creativity, colours, actions, emotions, etc. These enable us to recall better. Research says that 85 per cent of the time our brain visualizes in terms of images. Let's suppose that you are asked to imagine a bird or animal of your choice.

   While imagining, you are thinking of the image of a bird or an animal, not the spelling of that bird or animal. By this, it is clear that it is easier to remember any object, place or thing by its image rather than the spelling of that word.

2. **Associate**: A story should have a link, so that it can be memorized sequentially. Association can be based on colours, actions, dialogues or past experiences. For example, link only two words at a time, i.e., a parrot to a car, a car with a flower, a flower with a diary, a diary with a computer and so on. Create a story in this manner.

3. **The story should be bizarre**: A story should be strange, peculiar, funny, odd, curious, unconventional, unorthodox, unexpected, unfamiliar, abnormal, unusual, irregular, vivid, attractive, etc.

   The images should be absurd, unusual, out of the box as our brain distinguishes, prefers and encourages such visuals. For example, imagine that you are holding a zigzag-shaped building on your right finger. Such an image is distinguished by your brain, and hence, it is easy to remember since it is not a common activity.

Example: Let us associate two words: parrot and car
Simple story: A parrot is driving a car.
Bizarre story: Close your eyes and visualize a gigantic parrot driving the car at a speed of 100 km/hr. Use your senses to hear the sound of the car, imagine the speed of the vehicle and the huge parrot sitting inside it.

4. **Colours** play an important role in our life. Some colours are attractive, some are dull and some are close to our hearts. Use of coloured images in our memory help us identify them when required.
   Example: Car—Flowers
   Visualize a variety of flowers with vibrant colours blooming inside the car and their fragrance that make your day.

5. **Expand or shrink**: For example, if I tell you to imagine an elephant and you imagine a giant elephant walking on the streets, it might help you identify such an image immediately.
   For example: Flowers—Diary
   Visualize a very big diary made of the flowers blooming in the car.

6. **Senses** play a very important role—our eyes for watching movements, our ears for listening to the sounds, our nose for smelling, tongue for tasting and talking and skin for touch. The larger the senses involved in creating a story, the larger will be the possibilities of memorizing and recalling, since emotions are also attached to it.
   Example: Diary—Computer
   Apply all your senses—visualize that the diary is turning into a gigantic computer. Touch and feel it from all the sides, hear the sound by tapping on it and inhale the smell of the new computer.

7. **Emotions** such as happiness, sadness, anger, etc., affect our remembrance of any moment and help us recall the event.

Example: Computer—Chair

Imagine that the computer is resting on a chair in a peculiar posture. Making it a little funny can help recall better.

8. **2D/3D images**: The more dimensions you create, the easier it becomes to link and visualize. The image registers in your mind and makes recalling easy.

    Example: Chair—T-shirt

    Look at the picture of a T-shirt in different dimensions and notice how it looks from the top, the back, the front and sideways. Imagine the chair turning into a t-shirt. The different images can help you create your own image and register it in your mind.

9. **Your presence**: You can be present at any moment and at any linked point. It becomes easy to recall if you are associated with that object, person or place.

    Example: T-shirt—Watch

    Note the time it took for the chair to turn into a T-shirt. You are wearing a colourful, tough and milky watch. The image can connect to your mind strongly as you are involved in the current activity.

10. **Dialogues**: Add funny dialogues to make the story interesting and for easy remembrance. Dialogues can act as a catalyst.

    Example: Watch—Speaker

    Funny, catchy or famous dialogues play a very important role in connecting stories and for easy recall. Analysing what a particular object may say at a particular moment based on your experience and the scenes you have visualized play the right impact. For example, visualize the speaker grow a mouth and narrate Shah Rukh Khan's dialogue '*Puri kayanat...*'

11. **Life**: Add life to lifeless objects, create and visualize the story. Explore your imagination and add or modify the values and capabilities of that object.

Example: Speaker—Purse

The speaker starts talking to the purse. Add life to a purse. It visits places on its own and purchases whatever it wants. It throws away unwanted things such as cards, tickets, chits, etc., from it.

Note: The above points apply to only two consecutive words at a time in the complete sequence of words, i.e., to connect the first word with the second and the second with the third. One should disconnect the first word while associating the second with the third and so on.

When you connect two images, your brain connects the neurons. The connection point is called synapses. This happens very fast. When you perform the exercises, you only need to fix the images connected in about six seconds.

7.6: Tips: Creating Story

- Use positive, pleasant images. Your brain often blocks out the unpleasant ones.
- Use vivid, colourful, bizarre and sensible images—these are easier to remember.
- Use all your senses to code information or dress up an image. Remember that your mnemonic can contain sounds, smells, tastes, touch, movements and feelings as well as pictures.
- Give your image three dimensions, movements and space to make it more vivid. You can use movements to either maintain the flow of association or help you remember actions.
- Exaggerate the size of important parts of the image.
- Use humour! Funny or peculiar things are easier to remember than the normal ones.
- Similarly, rude rhymes are very difficult to forget!
- Symbols (red traffic lights, pointing fingers, road signs, etc.)

can encode quite complex messages quickly and effectively.

Now let us apply the rules for:

- Studying long answers in points for easy recall
- Memorizing a paragraph by underlying the important points
- Memorizing locations on the map sequentially

7.6.1. Activity: Association

Here are a few words. Use the rules taught to you and connect them.

For example:

Row 1: APPLE   CAR   INDIA
Simple story: An apple is in the car and the car is travelling all over India.
Creative story: Visualize a big apple and a dark red car coming out of the apple and moving at the maximum speed on the map of India.

Row 2: SPECS   CHAIR   MOTOR   PENCIL
Simple story:
Creative story:

Row 3: WALL   SPOON   TABLE   JAR
Simple story:
Creative story:

Row 4: CLOCK   PEN   BRUSH   CALCULATOR   ME
Simple story:
Creative story:

Row 5: TAB   BOOK   TABLA   BOX   RAJU
Simple story:
Creative story:

7.6.2: Activity: Story

Create a story from the following words. Visualize images of the following words one by one. Modify their shapes and sizes, relate them to each other in various combinations, and add life, colour and transparency. You can also draw and colour the image.

A teapot   A chair   An apple   A house   A bunch of flowers

Now apply all the above-mentioned rules that you have leaned and create a story.

Fill in the 'trained' column and assess the difference. Learn the use of the United Method for memorizing words in a sequence.

7.6.3: Activity: Use phrases

Create a story using the following phrases:

A boy with headphones on	A supercar
A goat in a forest	A magical brush
A barking dog	A bookworm
A glass of water	The traffic signal police
A dirty dress	Spanish noodles
Holiday mood	A boy crawling
A hungry tiger	Richie Rich
The busy Spiderman	Vegetable soup

7.6.4: Activity: Memorize

Remember the following words in sequence:

apple	car		India	
specs	chair	motor		pencil
wall		spoon	table	jar
clock	pen	brush	calculator	me
tab	book	tabla	box	Raju

Cover the table above and recall the words.

	car			
		motor		
				jar
			calculator	

7.7: Application in Studies

Aim: To analyse the results on the application of the United Method Technique.

Learning objective: To understand the proper application of the Power of 9.

What you need: Exercise sheet, ball point pen and colours.

What to do: Now create a new list and apply the United Method.

Students: Take a textbook and open the chapter you need to learn or study for your exams. Underline the important points and create a funny story and memorize the important points by using the **united method**. Recall during the next session.

Homemakers: Instead of making a shopping list, apply the skills to recall the items you need to buy.

7.8: Summary

Summarize what you have understood from this chapter—your takeaways—and how you would use it daily.

Chapter 8

Creativity

8.1: Introduction

Creativity is a process of producing new activity from our experiences, knowledge and learning by applying innovative ideas.

The dictionary defines **creativity** as the ability to transcend traditional ideas, rules, patterns, relationships and the like to create meaningful new ideas, forms, methods, interpretations, etc., to enhance originality, progressiveness or imagination.

One of the processes by which one utilizes creative ability is extensive reading.

8.1.1: Activity

Use the right side of your brain and think of as many **ideas** as you can to use the following items differently.

- Toothbrush
- Cleaning utensils
- Holder
- Hair dryer
- Dart
- Mobile
- Desk
- Pencil
- Flowers

From the above activity, we have channelized our thought processes and thinking from various angles, and have viewed the above items differently. Creativity deals with a **creative process** in the mind. To be creative, one needs to think consciously with a wider perspective and move from comfort zone to discomfort zone. Only then can creative skills be cultivated within us.

8.2: Creative Process

Let us understand the creative process and its many aspects.

8.2.1: Collaborate

Creativity involves collaboration of ideas, thoughts, brainstorming and acceptance of all ideas. Creative activities help the formation of new thoughts, ideas and the involvement of different minds to generate something new, unknown and acceptable.

8.2.1.1: Activity

A group of three or more students gets together and discusses the topic given: How to enjoy studying!

Come up with different ideas.

_____
_____
_____
_____
_____
_____

8.3.2: Regenerate

Neurons can generate and regenerate multiple effects and power if they are used properly. We need to rethink the issues of usage to dig out new innovative solutions. Logical thinking can be limited in terms of experience, regular habits and behaviours. Regeneration can help an individual come up with innovative ideas.

8.2.2.1: Activity: New ideas

Note down your bad habits and behaviours. Find out how you can overcome them by creating new and fresh ideas.

___

8.2.3: Exaggerate

We have the inherent potential to visualize the bigger picture in life and make the possibilities look bigger and better. Altering our vision beyond a certain limit creates a view better than the original size or shape as it broadens the scope of peripheral vision for better clarity.

8.2.3.1: Activity: Bigger and broader

Visualize and draw the following things bigger than their normal size and check the change for yourself:

Apple

___

Tiffin box

___

Cup and saucer

___

8.2.4: Ask questions

Tools for the generation of new ideas:

Ask 'what if?' and 'what else?' and you will find numerous answers popping in your brain.

8.2.4.1: Activity: What if...?

What if men start wearing saris?

___

8.2.5: Trigger

Anything can click at any moment. Perhaps you are sitting idle, working, or reading and something creeps into your mind and triggers your thoughts to change its usual direction and make things possible.

8.2.5.1: Activity: Jolt

Sit at a silent place and think of a problem in your life and its solution:

Note down the question below:

Wait for that jolt and ideas will nudge you forward.

8.2.6: Innovate

We don't create anything, we just modify. Innovation is a new method, idea or a product. Everything is created; we just need to modify as per today's requirement.

8.3: Statements That Kill Creativity

1. 'I have never tried it.'
2. 'Yeah! We had already tried that earlier.'
3. 'You have a point, but…'
4. 'It costs too much.'
5. 'That isn't your problem.'
6. 'We don't have time.'
7. 'Good idea, but it's impractical.'
8. 'That doesn't matter to you.'
9. 'You are ahead of your time.'
10. 'You can't teach an old dog new tricks.'
11. 'It won't work.'
12. 'Let's put that idea on the back-burner for now.'
13. 'We have always done it this way.'
14. 'It would take too much effort.'
15. 'Don't be a dreamer.'
16. 'Oh no! Not that idea again.'
17. 'Where did you dig that one up?'
18. 'We did fine without it before.'

8.4: Summary

Summarize what you have understood from this chapter—your takeaways—and how you would use it daily.

Chapter 9

Multiple Methods

9.1. Shape Method

Aim: To convert digits into images.

Learning objective: Numbers or alphabet are abstract and it's difficult to memorize and recall them at an appropriate time.

Create identical, abstract images taking into consideration the shape of the number and creating a new look by thinking and bringing your ideas to life.

What you need: An exercise sheet, a pencil and colours.

What to do: Look at the shape of the number and convert it to an object you identify with or an image other than a mathematical expression as shown in the example below.

Based on the shape of the digits, create an identical image.

Alphabet A means just a letter A, but it is easier to remember when visualized as an apple or an aeroplane. We can visualize an image and connect or associate it to the number as well.

Similarly, numbers 0–9 are abstract. They cannot be visualized in the form of images or it's not easy to associate them to remember them easily.

We are now going to learn different methods of converting abstract alphabets, numbers or objects in the form of easily understandable or viewable images for easy association.

9.1.1: Activity: Identify shapes

Observe the following figures and identify the images and numbers:

Tips: Identify numbers and images from the picture above.

_____
_____
_____
_____

9.1.2: Activity: Create shapes

0 : Ball ─────────────────────────────
1 : Pencil ───────────────────────────
2 : Duck ────────────────────────────
3 : Mountain ────────────────────────
4 : Chair ───────────────────────────
5 : Snake ───────────────────────────
6 : Elephant's trunk ────────────────
7 : Nose ────────────────────────────
8 : Snowman ─────────────────────────

9 : Lollipop

Now, think of your own images and draw them next to the numbers above.

9.1.3: How to use

Converting abstract numbers into shapes will enable you to effectively visualize them.

Instead of remembering the numbers, visualize the image and you will be able to associate them for better recall and remembrance.

Take a textbook and note down the important points of a long answer below and use the number-shape method to memorize the key points:

Number	Point	Create Story and link image of 1 to point 1
1		
2		
3		
4		
5		
6		
7		
8		
9		
10		

9.2: The *Main Hoon Na* Method

Aim: To understand the use of body parts.

Learning objective: How to use our body parts as links or to associate for easy remembrance.

What you need: An exercise sheet, a pencil and colours.

What to do: Identify our body parts in the sequence and list it down for further use.

The name of this section, '*main hoon na*', means, I am here! This system is purely based on the noting of sequence of parts from our hair to our toes. Each part resembles a point and the points can be easily connected with each part of the body.

Now let's get started:

रामरक्षा . मैं हूं ना	MHN
रामरक्षां पठेत्प्राज्ञः पापघ्नीं सर्वकामदाम् ।	.
शिरो मे राघवः पातु भालं दशरथात्मजः ॥ ४ ॥	Head . Forehead
कौसल्येयो दृशौ पातु विश्वामित्रप्रियः श्रुती ।	Eyes . Ears
घ्राणं पातु मखत्राता मुखं सौमित्रिवत्सलः ॥ ५ ॥	Nose . Mouth
जिह्वां विद्यानिधिः पातु कण्ठं भरतवन्दितः ।	Tongue . Throat
स्कन्धौ दिव्यायुधः पातु भुजौ भग्नेशकार्मुकः ॥ ६ ॥	Shoulders . Arms
करौ सीतापतिः पातु हृदयं जामदग्न्यजित् ।	Hands . Heart
मध्यं पातु खरध्वंसी नाभिं जाम्बवदाश्रयः ॥ ७ ॥	Midriff . Navel
सुग्रीवेशः कटी पातु सक्थिनी हनुमत्प्रभुः ।	Waist . Hips (Pockets)
ऊरू रघूत्तमः पातु रक्षःकुलविनाशकृत् ॥ ८ ॥	Thighs
जानुनी सेतुकृत्पातु जङ्घे दशमुखान्तकः ।	Knees . Shins
पादौ बिभीषणश्रीदः पातु रामोऽखिलं वपुः ॥ ९ ॥	Feet

9.2.1: Activity: Learn the parts

Observe parts of your body from your hair to your toes. On the left side of the table, you have the Sanskrit Ramraksha. Learn and note the sequence.

9.2.2: How to use

This way we can recall a long answer, paragraph, speech, etc.

9.3: Musical Walk

We are all very familiar with the place that we reside in, the path that we take to travel every day or the workplace where we spend most of our time at, say, a school, office, factory, etc.

This system helps you create memory landmarks in between the entry and exit points.

Let's **first** understand the difference between a usual walk and a musical walk.

- A usual walk is one wherein you walk as per your preferences and it may change depending upon the purpose of the walk.
- A musical walk is a set pattern where you assign the musical notes Sa, Re, Ga, Ma, Pa, Dha, Ni, Sa to each step you take.

Secondly,

- A usual walk need not have a purpose.
- Whereas, the name musical walk signifies that the walk is created in the musical format—Sa, Re, Ga, Ma, Pa, Dha, Ni…

Thirdly,

- A usual walk is without any set rules.
- Whereas, a musical walk has set rules, i.e., one must walk

from right to left or vice versa, or front to back or vis-a-vis.

9.3.1: Activity: Our house

L-R: Door, rack, mirror, kitchen utensils, cupboard, sofa, table, chair

Let us start creating a musical walk in your house. Select one room—the living room, study or the kitchen. Based on the set of rules, decide whether you want to start from right to left or left to right. Then, it's advisable to go from top to bottom. Normally, we first see objects at our eye level and then we look downwards.

9.3.2: How to use

This way we can recall one single long answer, paragraph, speech, etc., with objects in one room or a combination of two or more rooms.

List down all the objects that are fixed and immovable in your house. Each set of points resembles each object. This way you are aware about the known objects in a sequence, and they will help you connect with the desired answer.

For example, you need to recall the first point of the answer, which is 'climatic conditions do not favour tourism', and your first object in your house—'bell'. You need to connect 'climate' and 'tourism' with the object 'bell' (Story: Climate is too humid inside the bell. Hence, all the tourists are leaving the bell.)

This way you can remember points and in turn recall the answer.

1-10	11-20	21-30	31-40	41-50

9.3.3: Suggested musical walks

- Dentist
- Hospital
- Shopping mall, clothing stores
- Pharmacies
- Cinemas
- Gas stations
- Church, temple, mosque
- Kindergarten, schools, university
- Restaurants (Indian, Chinese, Japanese, etc.)
- Gym, tennis court, swimming pool
- Museum, art gallery
- Coffee Shops, McDonald's, Burger King
- Bars, clubs
- Bakeries
- Office
- Playgrounds
- Police station
- Car wash, garage
- Library
- Train stations, bus station, subway
- Post office

- Friend's and coworker's houses

9.4: Click Value Shape Rhyme (CVSR)

Aim: To differentiate between the various forms for easy distinction.

Learning objective: CVSR helps to memorize long formulas, equations and club different techniques together.

What you need: Book, a pencil and colour pens.

C stands for **Click**

Any word/object/scene/event that comes to your mind (clicks) when any particular number (0–9) is called out. For example: One—Thumb

V: Stands for **Value**

Any word/object/scene/event that has value (0–9). For example, One—or Ek—Eklavya, a One-Day match, etc.

S: Stands for **Shape**.

An appropriate shape which resembles a number (0–9). For example, One—stick, pen, pencil, pole, etc.

R: Stands for **Rhyme**.

Rhyming of the numbers (0–9) with words. For example, one—bun, gun, sun, etc.

9.4.1: Activity: Various forms

List down the memories that you find appropriate in the respective columns. Note that the number coincides with the memories.

No.	Click	Value	Shape	Rhyme
0				
1				
2				
3				

4				
5				
6				
7				
8				
9				
10				
11				
12				
13				
14				
15				
16				
17				
18				
19				
20				

9.4.2: How to use

You can use the CVSR in multiple ways. School students can use it to recall, fill in the blanks, match the columns, etc. Law and finance students can use it to recall sections and sub-sections.

You can either use CVSR or CVS or CV or just C. You can use this technique in multiple ways.

9.5: Ladder

Aim: To easily identify appropriate words and connect them to form a meaningful sentence as we climb up the ladder.
Learning objective: Definitions, paragraphs that a student needs to recall.

Multiple Methods • 103

What you need: A book, a pencil and colour pens.

Just as we climb the ladder, we put forward our steps and move ahead. It is important that meaningful words are put on each step and they are memorized, enabling us to learn long passages or definitions. 'Nouns' and 'Adjectives' can be the keywords to be imprinted on each step and the 'verbs' and connected words can be written next to them.

9.5.1: Activity

Write down the important points on the step and connecting words next them.

9.5.2: How to use

You can use this method to learn definitions, long answers, hierarchy, etc. This shall enable us to recall the words in the sequence.

9.6: Summary

Summarize what you have understood from this chapter—your takeaways—and how you would use it daily.

Chapter 10

Focus and Concentration

10.1: Introduction

Concentration is a tool necessary to accomplish a certain activity or assignment or a scheduled task. It creates a value-added tool to achieve your ultimate goal in life. Your idea is your soul and to keep it alive or to add life to it, you need to learn the art of concentration. Concentration is both art and science as it teaches us to work on a certain activity with utmost care.

We have more thoughts popping into our head than the minutes in a day. Without proper training, it becomes difficult to even hold on to a single thought. Do not be discouraged if you are unable to hold your thought on a subject for very long at first. You can overcome this tendency when you start reading and practising the contents provided below.

We have provided you with some activities below. If you just practise a few concentration exercises each day, you will notice positive changes in yourself.

10.2: Concentration

1. Concentration is the power of the mind, through fixed habit and practice, to keep your mind on one subject until you have thoroughly mastered it.
2. It may also mean the ability to throw off the effects of habits which you wish to discard, and power to build new habits that are more to your liking. It means complete self-mastery.

3. Concentration is the ability to think as you wish to think; the ability to control your thoughts and direct them to a definite end; it is the ability to organize your knowledge into a plan of action that is sound and workable.
4. Ambition and desire are the chief factors, which enter into the act of successful concentration.
5. Desire what you may, and if your desire is within reason and if it is strong enough, the power of concentration will help you attain it.
6. Nothing was ever created by a human being which was not first created in the imagination, through desire and then transformed into reality through concentration.
7. When you concentrate on a particular project, the facts closely related to that project will 'pour' in from every conceivable source. The theory is that a deep-seated desire to accomplish a project, when once planted in the right sort of 'mental soil', serves as a centre of attraction or magnet that attracts to it everything that harmonizes with the nature of the desire.
8. Learn to fix your attention on a given subject, at will, for whatever length of time you choose, and you will have learned the secret passageway to power and plenty. This is concentration.
9. There are a few causes that will make your mind wander— physical illness, shock, accident, restlessness, indolence, lack of interest, morbid anxiety, habit of drifting, monotony of daily work, highly specialized duties narrowing the mental sphere, etc. It is necessary to attend only to a few subjects to do well in them. Narrow your range and intensify your focus.
10. Trace the cause of your mind wandering and follow a stringent method of work so as to enable yourself to concentrate on one thing at a time for at least half an hour.
11. If you want to develop extraordinary memory, it is necessary

to develop the power of concentration. You cannot recall what you have never concentrated on. If the original experience is vague, the result will be vague. If you sow in attention, you must not look for a rich harvest of recollections. If your mind wanders, you get a mass of vague and unorganized data. Let your mind concentrate, and the mass will change into a classified and easily recollected whole.

Discovery and originality are the results of concentration. No man gets brilliant and original ideas about which he has thought little and of which he knows nothing at all.

10.2.1: Activity: Concentration

Prepare Yourself
Settle down in a calm place where you feel comfortable.

Light a candle and place it about one metre in front of you. Sit cross-legged on the floor and put a small cushion under yourself if necessary or on a chair, in a comfortable position, your back straight against the back of the chair and your legs apart and relaxed. If the seating position isn't comfortable, stretch out on the floor for five minutes if conditions permit. Close your eyes and call to your mind each part of your body so that you can then relax that part. Breathe calmly and deeply while you work your way through your whole body.

Relax
Remain in this position, with your eyes closed, for several minutes, being aware of your body and its stability. Be aware of the rhythm of your breathing that becomes calmer and more regular.

Now, focus on the flame. If your thoughts try to move in other directions, bring them slowly back to the flame. Relax your facial muscles.

Close your eyes slowly
Breathe deeply, paying attention to your breathing, and feel your stomach rising and falling as you inhale and exhale. This abdominal breathing encourages relaxation.

Take your time breathing in and out slowly, and let yourself slip into this regular rhythm as though you're being rocked on the waves. Repeat silently to yourself, 'I am calm; I am relaxing', until you feel completely calm. If you still feel some tension in your muscles, make use of this rhythmic breathing to help yourself relax them. Feel a sense of calmness flow into you.

Conjure up in your mind a picture of the flame. Remain focussed on its never-ending movements. It occupies your whole mind. It is as though you are hypnotized by its dancing motion and by its colours. When a thought comes to mind again, let it come, then let it be consumed by the flame.

10.2.2: Activity: Find all 'F's
Circle all the Fs in the following extract.

- Our brain is an extremely complex network of cells called NEURONS. It consists of billions of neurons. They send in information in the form of electrical and chemical signals to another neuron through a bridge—synapse. When any information is passed on, the neurons connect the information and store it for future use with the help of synapse. The information is stored either in form of electrical signal (verbal communication) and Chemical signals (emotions).

Our attention span and interest in learning decides whether the information will be stored in

- Short-term Memory (STM)
- Mid-term memory (MTM)

- Long-term Memory (LTM)

The largest part of brain is called cerebral cortex.
The cerebral cortex is divided into lobes, each having a specific function. Most of the information processing occurs in the cerebral cortex.
The neocortex is divided into four major lobes—the frontal lobe, the parietal lobe, the temporal lobe and the occipital lobe.
Frontal Lobe—Helps in speaking, planning, comparing, abstract thinking.
Parietal Lobe—Processes visuals, auditory and touch information.
Occipital Lobe—The back of the brain helps to store information related to sight.
Temporal Lobe—Helps in comprehension, sound and speech.

Tip: When you emphasize on the phonetic sound, you can identify the sound and its form or picture.

10.2.3: Activity: How much attention do you pay
Try and recall the brands/number/size of the following things in your house.

In the Bathroom: Brand
Soap ─────────────────────────
Toothpaste ─────────────────────
Perfume ────────────────────────
Shampoo ────────────────────────
Buckets (how many) ──────────────
Toothbrush ─────────────────────
Razor ──────────────────────────
Mirror (size) ───────────────────

In the House:

Washing Machine ————————————
Television ——————————————
Camera ————————————————
Iron ——————————————————
Hair Dryer ——————————————

- Name five shops in your area.
- Do you know the make of the car or scooter of three of your family members or neighbours?

10.2.4: Exercises

- Here are three good exercises that can help you create a strong, clear focus, and of course, these are solutions to how you can improve concentration.

1) **Strengthen concentration.**
    - Twice a day, practise holding a specific object in your mind steadily. The item should have some detail that you can imagine, but it should also be simple to 'see' it in your mind. Some good examples: an apple, a pencil, the face of your pet, your house as it looks from the outside, and so on. Choose something you won't have trouble picturing, but something that requires you to focus in order to see it clearly.
    - Call up a strong mental image of it, and then try to keep your focus on the object for a full five or ten minutes without losing your focus. This is hard to do at the beginning because your mind is probably untrained. Random thoughts and pictures may keep popping up in your mind and you'll have to keep pulling your attention back to the object again. Don't let this stop you! Remember, the only reason you struggle with this is because you don't have a strong ability to focus yet.

As you keep working at it daily, you'll notice that you find it easier and easier to concentrate with time.
- The stronger your ability to concentrate during your focus sessions, the more you'll notice you're not having trouble concentrating at other times either. Could this be the first major step in how to improve concentration?

2) **Empty your mind.**

Another focus-killer is a head full of scattered thoughts. You know those days when you've got a million things going on and you're trying to remember them all at once and you keep forgetting things anyway? Emptying your mind can do wonders for scattered thoughts!

- Before you do this exercise, first make a list of everything you can think of that you need to remember. This will help you feel more comfortable about releasing your scattered thoughts.
- Then, set aside five or ten minutes to focus on quieting your thoughts.
- Though this exercise is called 'empty your mind', you really can't completely empty your mind of thoughts. Your thoughts will keep on flowing through your mind the whole time. However, you can detach and simply let them pass by. You become an observer of sorts, watching your thoughts flow by. You're aware that you're having thoughts, but you don't latch on to them and start 'thinking' actively about them. You simply sit in a space of peace while your thoughts flow calmly past. This experience is hard to describe, but once you master it, you'll have discovered a powerful technique for releasing stress and improving your focus in a very short time! How to improve concentration tips might be easy at first sight, but they are much more difficult to practise.

3) Visualize for practice.

If you've got an important goal or task coming up and you're feeling unsure about your ability to do it, visualize it first! Many studies have been done on the power of visualization, and the general consensus is that performing tasks and activities mentally over and over again is equally effective as performing them physically! That means that visualization can serve as a powerful practice session that helps you master anything, including better time management! Try visualizing yourself staying balanced, calm and focussed throughout the course of your day, easily handling any surprises and interruptions, and feeling happy and proud of yourself at the end of the day. Visualize yourself giving a successful speech, getting better at sports activities, or anything else you want to master. The trick is to go through it completely in your own mind, seeing and feeling what you would see and feel while it's really happening. The more you do this the more proficient you will become at it and the more you'll start seeing results in your physical activities.

10.3: Focus

Sharply locking your sight on an object leading to concentration creates **focus**. Students at any given time need to focus on the words and visualize the contents to understand the context of the information. A focussed approach can help to understand, learn and recall at a given amount of time.

10.3.3: Foods that are good for eyesight

1. Carrots
2. Eggs
3. Milk
4. Apricots

5. Berries
6. Black currants
7. Cold-water fishes
8. Collard greens
9. Grapefruits
10. Grapes
11. Lemons
12. Spinach
13. Fish oils

10.3.4: Activity: Activate your curiosity and imagination

Pick a magazine and find photos of several people. Then, look at them and make a story.

Or turn off the sound of the TV programme and try to read their lips or understand what they are saying from their gestures and facial expressions.

10.3.5: Activity: Mirror game

See in the mirror and answer the questions:

- Which is higher—right eyebrow or left?
- Which of your eyes is bigger and brighter—right or left?
- Which of your hands is bigger—right or left?
- Which side of yourself is more balanced—right or left?

10.4: Summary

Summarize what you have understood from this chapter—your takeaways—and how you would use it daily.

Chapter 11

Vedic Maths

11.1: Introduction

The ancient system of Vedic Mathematics was rediscovered from the Indian Sanskrit texts known as the Vedas, between 1911 and 1918 by Sri Bharati Krsna Tirthaji (1884–1960). At the beginning of the twentieth century, when there was a great interest in the Sanskrit texts in Europe, Bharati Krsna spoke of some scholars who ridiculed certain texts called *Ganita Sutras,* meaning Mathematics. They could find no Mathematics in the translation and dismissed the texts as utter rubbish. Bharati Krsna, who was himself a scholar of Sanskrit, Mathematics, History and Philosophy, studied these texts. After a lengthy and careful investigation, he was able to reconstruct the Mathematics of the Vedas.[1]

Let us see below how we can enjoy or work with Mathematics using the Vedic system rediscovered by Tirthaji.

11.2: Addition

Let us start with addition:

Usually, when a student is asked to add the following figures:

$$3 \quad 9$$
$$4 \quad 2$$

---

[1] http://www.vedicmaths.org/introduction/history

$$\begin{array}{cc} 5 & 7 \\ 6 & 9 \end{array}$$

...he or she goes on logically adding the units place, the tens and solves the sum. There are chances that he may lose track and increase or decrease one point. For example, let us add the numbers: $9 + 2 = 11$, $11 + 7 = 18$, $18 + 9 = 27$. Here, the carryover is 2, but in haste, a student may assume the sum as 37/17 (by oversight).

Vedic Maths has been discovered to eliminate such errors. It uses the safest method by adding only the first 10 digits repeatedly.

Say, $9 + 2 = 11$, now drop 10 points (indicating a DOT near digit 2). Now, move forward with additional $1 + 7 + 9$ till you don't get a 10.

$$\begin{array}{cc} 3 & 9 \\ 4 & 2 \end{array}$$

($1 + 7 + 9 = 17$) Now, leave 10 points (indicating a DOT near digit 9). So now, we have 2 dots indicating carry forward of 2 points.

$$\begin{array}{cc} 4 & 1 \\ 5 & 7 \\ \underline{4} & \underline{9} \\ & 7 \end{array}$$

The dot indicates 10, so you are leaving 10 and moving forward with the one digit numbers. Same process can be used for tens. This simplifies the process of big calculations, wherein students are likely to make mistakes are eliminated.

This helps the students to do their sums faster and with more accuracy and ease.

11.2.1: Activity: Add the following numbers

```
  7 9
  4 4
  6 8
  ───
  3 5
```

11.2.2: Digit sum

Suppose you want to check if the following addition is correct.

```
  4 3
  3 2 +
  ───
  7 5
```

We find the digit sums of 43, 32 and 75 and check that the first two digit sums add up to the third digit sum.

```
  4 3      7
  3 2 +    5 +
  ───     ───
  7 5      3
```

The digit sums are shown on the right and
7 + 5 = 3 is correct in digit sums because
7 + 5 = 12 = 3 (1 + 2 = 3)

This indicates that the answer is correct.

All sums, even the most complex, can be checked in this way.

Use this easy method of adding numbers to check your bank statement or supermarket bill.

The usual way to add numbers works from right to left, and so is not useful for mental maths. Numbers are written and spoken from left to right. So, it is easier to work from left to right, especially when doing it in your mind.

- 34 + 52 = 86
  This is easy to do from left to right.
  We add 3 and 5 to get 8.
  And we add 4 and 2 to get 6.

You can use the digit sum method to check these.
Now suppose that there is a over carry figure.

- 76 + 86 = 162
  The figures on the left add up to 7 + 8 = 15.
  The figures on the right add up to 6 + 6 = 12.
  1 5 12 = 1 6 2

Now, as 12 is a 2-digit number, the 1 will be carried over to turn the 15 into 16, giving us 162.

This can be easily done in your mind—for any two-figure number, carry the left-hand figure to the left.

- 373 + 474 = 847
  First we get 7.
  Then we get 14: 714 = 84.
  Finally we get 7 which gives 847.

11.3: Subtraction

Use the formula **all from 9 and the last from 10** to perform instant subtractions.

- For example, 1000 − 357 = 643
- We simply subtract the first two figures in 357 from 9 and the last figure from 10.

```
1  0  0  0   -    3    5    7
                  |    |    |
              from 9 from 9 from 10
                  ↓    ↓    ↓
           =      6    4    3
```

So, the answer is 1000 − 357 = 643

This always works for subtractions from numbers consisting of a 1 followed by naught: 100; 1000; 10,000 etc.

- Similarly, 10,000 − 1049 = 8951

```
1  0,  0  0  0   -   1    0    4    9
                     |    |    |    |
                 from 9 from 9 from 9 from 10
                     ↓    ↓    ↓    ↓
             =       8    9    5    1
```

- For 1000 − 83, in which we have more zeros than figures in the numbers being subtracted, we simply suppose 83 is 083.

  So, 1000 − 83 becomes 1000 − 083 = 917.

11.3.1: Activity: Subtraction

10,000 − 2457

1,000 − 478

10,000 − 7239

100 − 34

1000 − 398

11.3.2: Even and odd numbers

Now let us work out the subtraction for odd numbers:

```
    5  7  4  2
 -  3  1  7  6
   ─────────────
    2  5  6  6
```

Some of the students **fear** subtraction, but not addition. So here, let us use addition for doing the subtractions.

```
Th H T U
 5 7 4 2
 3 1 7 6
 6 8 2 4
 ───────
 2 5 6 6
```

Working of the 3rd row:

    For the units place 6, to become 10, you need to add 4.
    For 7 in the tens place to become 9, you need to add 2.
    For 1 in the hundreds place to become 9, you need to add 8.
    For 3 in the thousands place to become 9, you need to add 6.
    Now, here we shall be adding the 1st row + 3rd row.
    Units place: 2+4 = 6
    Tens place: 4+2 = 6
    Hundreds place: 7+8 = 15
    Here the carry over shall be subtracted, so 5 − 1 = 4
    Thousands place shall be 6 − 4 = 2
    You get the answer as 2 5 6 6........

11.3.3: Activity

Let us take another example:

```
   Th H T U
    7 9 4 5
  − 5 8 6 2
    4 1 3 8
    ───────
    2 0 8 3
```

Working of the 3rd Row:

    For the units place 2, to become 10, you need to add 8.
    For 6 in the tens place, to become 9, you need to add 3.
    For 8 in the hundreds place to become 9, you need to add 1.
    For 5 in the thousands place to become 9, you need to add 4.
    Now here, we shall add the first row + third row.

Units place: 5 + 8 = 13

Now the 1 to be added to the tens place (4 +1) = 5

tens place: 5 + 3 = 8

Hundreds place: 9 + 1 = 10

Here, the carry over shall be subtracted since it's the greatest number in the series,

So, 7 − 1 = 6

Thousands place shall be 6 − 4 = 2

You get the answer, 2 5 6 6.

11.4: Multiplication

For one, two and multiple numbers, the multiplication technique differs.

Let us start with single-digit numbers.

11.4.1: Single digit

Don't know your tables? Never mind! In this system you don't need them beyond 5 × 5!

- Suppose you need 8 × 7

    8 is 2 is less than 10 and 7 is 3 is less than 10.

    Think of it like this:

    ```
    8   2
    7   3
    ─────
    5   6   answer
    ```

    The answer is 56.

    The diagram below shows how you get it.

    ```
    8   2
      × |
    7   3
    ─────
    5   6   answer
    ```

You subtract crosswise 8-3 or 7−2 to get 5, the first

figure of the answer.
And you multiply vertically: 2 × 3 to get 6, the last figure of the answer.

That's all you do.

See how far the numbers are below 10, subtract one number's deficiency from the other number, and multiply the deficiencies together.

- $7 \times 6 = 42$

$$\begin{array}{cc} 7 & 3 \\ \times & | \\ 6 & 4 \\ \hline 3 & {}_12 \end{array} = \mathbf{42}$$

Here there is a carry over: The 1 in the 12 goes over to make 3 into 4.

11.4.2 : Two digits

- Suppose you want to multiply 88 by 98.
  By calculating vertically and diagonally, you can immediately get the answer, using the same method as before.
  Both 88 and 98 are close to 100.
  88 is 12 is less than 100 and 98 is 2 is less than 100.
  You can imagine the sum set out like this:

$$\begin{array}{cc} 88 & -\ 12 \\ \times & | \\ 98 & -\ 2 \\ \hline 86 & 24 \end{array}$$

As done before, 86 comes from subtracting crosswise: 88 − 2 = 86 (or 98 − 12 = 86: you can subtract either way, you will always get the same answer). And the 24 in the answer is just 12 × 2: you multiply vertically. So 88 × 98 = 8624

This is so easy that it is just mental arithmetic.

11.4.3: Magical squares

Ending with 5:

$75^2 = \mathbf{5625}$

75^2 means 75×75.

The answer is in two parts: 56 and 25.

The last part is always **25**.

The first part is the first number, 7, multiplied by the number 'one more', which is 8:

so, $7 \times 8 = 56$

$7 \quad 5^2 \quad = \quad 5 \quad 6 \quad 2 \quad 5$

$7 \times 8 = 56$

Try yourself:

$25 \times 25 =$

$45 \times 45 =$

$65 \times 65 =$

$85 \times 85 =$

$105 \times 105 =$

11.4.4: Same first digit

- $32 \times 38 = 1216$

   Both numbers here start with 3 and the last figures (2 and 8) add up to 10.

   So we just multiply 3 by 4 (the next number up) to get 12 for the first part of the answer.

   And we multiply the last digits: $2 \times 8 = 16$ to get the last part of the answer.

Diagrammatically:

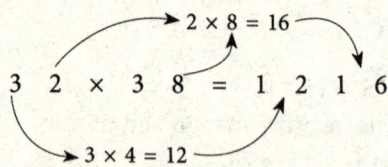

- And 81 × 89 = 7209
  Try this:
  47 × 43 =
  61 × 68 =

11.4.5: Multiplying by 11

Multiplying a number by 11 is incredibly easy. Astonish your parents and friends with the following technique.

To multiply any two-digit number by 11 we just put the total of the two figures between the 2 figures.

- 26 × 11 = 286

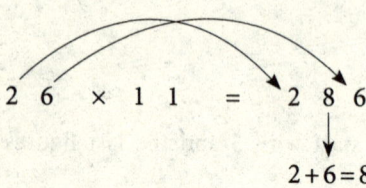

Notice that the outer figures in 286 are the 26 being multiplied.

And the middle figure is just 2 and 6 added up.
- So 72 × 11 = 792
- 77 × 11 = 847
  This involves a carry over figure because 7 + 7 = 14 we get 77 × 11 = 7147 = 847.
  234 × 11 = 2574

We put the 2 and the 4 at the ends.
We add the first pair 2 + 3 = 5.
and we add the last pair: 3 + 4 = 7.

Try this:

$$34 \times 11 =$$
$$298 \times 11 =$$
$$123 \times 11 =$$

11.5: Summary

Summarize what you have understood from this chapter—your takeaways—and how you would use it daily.

Chapter 12

Brain Mapping

12.1: Introduction

This technique can help in compressing the information, making it easy and forming information into visual images. A brain map is a diagrammatic representation to represent words, ideas, tasks or other items linked to and arranged around a central key word or idea.

Creative Brain mapping is a graphical representation of images, shapes, colours, symbols, routes, etc. It's a simple method of putting the notes artistically. Visuals help one to distinguish words or ideas. It, generally, takes a hierarchical tree or branch format. Brain mapping allows greater creative and imaginative skills. It also allows the brain to associate words with visual representation. Graphical representation helps the brain to focus on individual road maps, routes or branches and helps in proper understanding.

A structured network has modelling relationships, with coloured lines and objects connecting with each other to show association and a relationship between them.

12.2: Most Common Style of Note-taking

Most of the common styles of note-taking and note-making, and all in one colour is known as **monotone**.

Monotone = NOT Brain-friendly.

Brain Mapping • 125

And, all these traits come from, predominantly, the left side of the brain.

What about the right side of the brain?

A much better way to process our thoughts is to make a Creative map!

12.3: Purpose

Aim: To create charts, memory images, blocks, creative representation of study material, content, etc.

Learning objective: Tools, techniques and exercises

What you need:

- Plain white paper—good quality A4- or A3-sized
- Cardboard
- Coloured pens
- Pencils
- Highlighters
- Eraser
- Textbook
- Ideas

Pencils that are usually used will help, but **coloured** pens work best.

12.4: Activity: Learn to Draw

Take an A4-sized paper. Hold a pencil in your hand.

- Start drawing by moving the pencil
- Then, only with your fingers
- Again, only with your wrist
- Next, only with your elbow
- Finally, only with your arms

12.5: Benefits

Brain maps are used to generate, visualize, structure and classify ideas. They are an aid to studying and organizing information, solving problems, making decisions and writing.

What can we use brain maps for?

- Note-taking
- Brainstorming (individually or in groups)
- Problem-solving
- Studying and memorizing
- Planning
- Researching
- Presenting information
- Gaining insight on complex subjects
- Using your creativity

Creative brain maps can be used for:

- Solving any critical problem
- Finalizing any design layout
- Structure/relationship representations
- Collaboration
- Combination of words and visuals/imagination/creativity/sound/colours
- Expression of creativity
- Team-building or synergy-creating activity
- Enhancing work culture and morale

12.6: Process

1. Start at the centre with an image of the topic, using at least two to three colours.
2. Use images, symbols, colours, codes, and two or three dimensions throughout your brain map.

3. Select key words and use upper or lowercase letters—if possible, write using different coloured pens.
4. Each word or image is best left alone and sitting on its own line.
5. The lines should be connected, starting from the central image. The central lines are thicker, organic and thinner as they move out from the centre.
6. Make the lines the same length as the word/image they support.
7. Use multiple colours throughout the mind map, for visual stimulation and also to encode or group.
8. Develop your own personal style of brain mapping.
9. Show associations in your brain map.

Keep the brain map clear by using radial hierarchy, numerical order or outlines to embrace your branches

12.7: Activity: Drawing a Brain Map

Take a plain sheet of paper. Start from the centre and create a brain map of yourself. It includes your education, hobbies, likes, dislikes, experiences, etc.

You can create a creative brain mapping of movies you have seen or heard about. The types of movies could be romantic, thriller, comedy, action, cartoon, horror, etc. Use the following questions:

- What kinds of movies do you like most?
- Why do you like them?
- Which are your favourite movies?
- Why did you enjoy the movie?

12.8: Summary

Summarize what you have understood from this chapter—your takeaways—and how you would use it daily.

Chapter 13

Vocabulary Builder

13.1: Introduction

One of the biggest hurdles in learning a new language is **vocabulary**.

A lot of people want to know how they can learn a language. The best way to learn is to learn its vocabulary. When I was learning Deutsche, I learned the vocabulary first, then the verbs, nouns, adjectives, etc., and then how to form sentences.

13.2: Activity: Alphabet Game

Alphabet	Name	Place/Town	Animal/Bird	Thing/Object	Country
A					
D					
G					
M					
N					
P					
S					
T					

Vocabulary Builder • 129

Tips: Association of the names of places, animals and objects to connect with verbal memory.

13.3: Basic Vocabulary Rules

Rule. No. 1: When you come across a new word, repeat, repeat, repeat! Everyone has a different way of learning. If you are a visual learner, you would first write the word and then draw corresponding images and try to connect with the meaning. If you are an auditory learner, you will learn the languages faster.

Rule. No. 2: You can have posters or sticky notes. Write the words down and stick on things you mostly use. For example, your cupboard, study desk, etc.

Each word conveys a meaning. Words are used as tools to communicate feelings, expressions, messages etc. The ingredients are mixed in proportions and then communicated via signals. The response is recorded as per the expression or the mode of transfer of information.

Rule No. 3: Whenever you wish to create something out of words, play with the raw alphabets, words or sentences, and hurray! The magic happens.

Rule No. 4: Find the root from where the word originates, because that helps to understand better. Create a visual reference that nails down the pronunciation.

13.4: Activity: Senses

Can you recall from your experience what comes to your mind when you say that something is soft or slimy? Note them down below.

Soft:	Slimy:	Textured:

Tip: How fast do you respond to the senses of touch and sound, and how do they stimulate your senses?

13.5: Creative Vocab Technique

Whenever we need to study a new word—to know the meaning, translate into another language or to learn a new language—we need to first be able to pronounce that word. Phonetics help us to pronounce accurately.

The second step is to try to analyse the word and use one of the following:

Substitute: What other word in either your mother tongue or any other known language can be used instead of what has been used?

Connect: What can be connected to the word so that a meaningful dialogue can be created?

Combine: What else can be combined to create something new and remarkable or easy to remember?

Adjust: How can you add more character to a word to remember it?

Absorb: What can it absorb to perform a new function?

Magnify: How can you enlarge its scope, i.e., how can you apply your creative skills to make it more visible?

Use: What other uses can you think of for it?

Eliminate: What can you eliminate or remove to form a meaningful and understandable word to remove any confusion?

Reverse: What can be done upside down, back to front?

Rearrange: How can you reconfigure the words in a given group of words?

This technique can be used for:

- Learning new words—easy memorizing and recall
- Learning any foreign language
- Identifying comparative words, expressions
- Substituting to create word-list and increase vocabulary

13.6: Activity: Holiday Memories

For creative visualization, create memory images for easy recall.

Holiday memories pertaining to each of your senses:

Write down from your memory about the last vacation you had with your family and friends, or a social event: ———

Places / Location:	

Tip: Mental images triggered from any event, which are related to the senses.

13.7: Creative Vocabulary Rules

1. You need to create a story link between words and the meanings of the words or associate with each other and make it funnier.
2. It is easy to remember and recall any sequence in the form of a story and images (creative and imaginative). Suppose, here, I tell you to imagine any bird or animal of your choice (say peacock, parrot, lion or tiger).

While imagining a bird or an animal for instance, you must imagine the bird or animal and not the spelling. By this, it is easy to remember any object, place or thing by its image rather than the spelling of that word.
3. The images should be absurd, vivid, bizarre or any impossible thing happening around you, for example, visualize a big fat mouse scolding a cat who is shrinking. Our brain accepts such imaginations, making them easier for recall.
4. Colours play an important role in our life. Some colours are attractive, some are dull and some are close to our heart. Use of coloured images in our memory helps us to identify them when required.
5. Imagining big objects in a smaller size, and small objects in a bigger size again becomes an absurdity. For example, if I tell you to imagine an aeroplane, and if you imagine a giant aeroplane being carried by an ant, it shall help you remember such an image immediately.
6. Senses play a very important role—eyes to see, ears to listen to sounds, nose to smell, tongue to taste and skin to touch. The more the senses are involved in creating a story, the more are the possibilities of memorizing and recalling, since the emotions are also attached to it.
7. Emotions such as happiness, sadness, anger, etc., affect our remembrance of any moment and helps to recall the event.
8. Add dialogues as backup wherever possible to make the link memorable.

13.8: Tips

- Use positive, pleasant images while connecting or associating words. Your brain often blocks out unpleasant ones.
- Use colourful, sensible and regular images—these are easier to remember.

Vocabulary Builder • 133

- Use all your senses to encode and decode information or form an image from your memory. Remember that your mnemonic can contain sounds, smells, tastes, touch, movements and feelings and overall it should display as a single picture.
- Give your image three dimensions, movement and space to make it more meaningful. You can use actions or movements to maintain the flow of association, which can help you to recall easy.
- Shrink or exaggerate the size of important parts of the image.
- Use humour! Funny, unusual or peculiar things are easier to remember than normal ones.
- Similarly, rude rhymes or sensitive images are very difficult to forget!
- Symbols (red traffic lights, pointing fingers, road signs, etc.) can code quite complex messages quickly and effectively.

13.9: Activity: Identify Products

Identify the products that correspond with the taglines and add which senses were activated:

Visual (V), Auditory (A), Touch (To), Taste (Ts), Smell (S)... Tick mark ☑ wherever applicable √

Sr. No	Keywords/Image/Hint	PRODUCT	V	A	To	Ts	S
1	*Daag Ache Hai*		√	√			√
2	*Zuban Pe Lagaam*						
3	*The Mint with the Hole*						
4	*Maa Ne Banaye Hai*						
5	*Maa Ki Yaad Aa Gai*						
6	*Because You're Worth It*						
7	*Taste the Thunder*						
8	*Do Ghoot Ki Baat Hai*						

Tip: Mental images that trigger words you have heard are related to the senses.

13.10: Vocab: Method One

By using the creative vocabulary technique one can use the words and meaning and transform them into creative images based on experience and vocabulary.

Let us start with the activity:

Word: _____ Origin: _____
Meaning: _____

Substitute	
Connect	
Combine	
Adjust	
Absorb	
Magnify	
Use	
Eliminate	
Reverse	
Rearrange	

You can also draw symbols or create a memory image which can help you memorize or visualize the word along with its meaning and reproduce it when necessary.

The definition of the word can be brought to life via comparison, symbols, links, expressions and memory images. The links make powerful associations and the more you apply bizarre thinking, it helps to learn the selected word with ease, and makes the association stronger.

13.10.1: Example

Word: EDIFY   Origin: Middle English

Meaning: To build up, establish, strengthen a person, institution, to uplift

Substitute	Edi (Murphy)
Connect	FY (Flying)
Combine	Edi (Murphy) + FY (Flying) + meaning
Adjust	
Absorb	
Magnify	Visualize Edi Murphy Flying
Use	Creative imagination—right side of brain
Eliminate	
Reverse	
Rearrange	Why? To build up/to uplift

13.11: Vocab: Method Two

You can use a flash card for each word:

Front:

```
SUBSTITUTE              ADJUST
CONNECT                 ABSORB
COMBINE
              WORD

MAGNIFY                 ELIMINATE
USE                     REVERSE
```

Back:

```
┌─────────────────────────┐
│                         │
│                         │
│        MEANING          │
│                         │
│                         │
└─────────────────────────┘
```

13.11.1: Making sight word flash cards

To make sight word flash cards, all you need are index cards. Ideally, three by five inches. You can use index cards that are lined or ones without lines. I would definitely recommend that if the child writes the flash card, use lined index cards. If you're an adult, a pen is sufficient, or if you want to make it more salient, you can use a marker. If the child writes that flash card, I definitely recommend that he or she should use a pencil. When you make a sight word flash card, it's important that your print is one is lowercase, and that each letter is approximately two to three inches.

13.11.2: Playing games with sight words

What better way to teach sight words to kids than through games? In this exercise, I've decided to use three sight words and I've duplicated each sight word on a total of six index cards. So, what we're going to do is flip over two cards and we're going to try to match the sight words.

What does this say? 'Where, where...' Nice. Can you find the word here? There you go. Find the word 'said'. So, one convenient way to practise sight words is to place the sight words index cards on a ring and place the ring in a folder, and to have a sheet of loose-leaf paper that's lined, and this sheet can be used by the child to practise writing the sight word.

13.12: Tips for Creative Vocabulary

Whenever we need to study a new word, we must either get the meaning, translate it into another language or learn a new sequence of new words memorization

1. Write the new word, its pronunciation and the translation into English.
2. Recall only 'images–senses' of the words, paying particular attention to a thorough selection of visual images.
3. While memorizing, listen to the pronunciation of the word and repeat those loudly in the background of image-sense in your imagination.
4. Perform control recall and distinguish words whose pronunciation should be memorized by means of auxiliary images.
5. Memorize difficult words, using combination of similar sounding English words and phonetic symbols.
6. Repeat words by heart in any spare time you have.

13.13: Activity: Replace Alphabet

Replace only one alphabet in each of the following words in order to arrive at a new meaningful word. Let us see how many words you can think of (no interchange of alphabets).

maid		fine		mate	
bun		fix		plane	
south		dear		rose	
invert		crack		pine	
post					

Hint: Use your logic and recall from your memory/use rhyming words).

13.14: Sequence Memorization

There is no need to have many support images for memorizing a sequence of new foreign words. After the connection between image-sense and word pronunciation is fixed, support images can be used repeatedly.

Let us say that you have memorized fifty new words. Words can be memorized quite fast. Even if you spend only one minute per new word, then you will be able to memorize about fifty words per hour. This is the actual time required for qualitative memorizing.

Important!

- It is not possible to speed up the development of a connection between different analysers; the process of strengthening a group of new words or phrases should be divided during a minimum of four days.
- Do not attempt to learn a song's lyrics in one day. In the first day you will capture phrases and may be able to deliver a tentative reproduction. You will need at least four days to be able to automatically reproduce text without thinking. During that time the text should be repeated continuously. The same goes for a group of new words.
- If you need to retell a text on Friday, you need to memorize it on Monday.

To develop a connection between a visual image and a word pronunciation, you need to activate this connection over a couple of days.

Imagine and pronounce an image over a period. This should be done with all words and only by heart. If you memorize fifty words today, then tomorrow you will need to exercise them in your imagination to form the connection 'image—pronunciation'.

The next day, you will need ten new support images for memorizing a new group of words.

On the third day, you will have to memorize ten more new words but continue exercising your imagination of the first and second group.

On the fourth day, you will have to memorize ten more new words but continue exercising your imagination of the first, second and third group.

On the fifth day, you will be able to memorize new words on the first fifty support images.

Note:

- You do not have to memorize ten to fifteen new words every day. You can memorize one group of words and repeat them for several days. After strengthening a group of words in your memory, you can memorize the next group. If you memorize twenty new words every three days—it is 200 words per month. Not bad! You can start to read children's books. For this, you will need 50-100 support images.

13.15: Choosing Sight Words

A sight word vocabulary is a store of words a student can identify and/or read automatically. They know the word by sight. They do not need to sound out the word. Sight words should include high frequency words, which are words commonly used in every day conversation and common words you see in print. One of the best sources to find sight words is from the Dolce word list. You can actually get it online for free. Learning these 220 words can help a child read approximately 50–75 per cent of what is printed in almost any piece of children's literature.

13.16: Activity: Create Words

Delete/replace/add one letter (once you change it, keep the first letter intact) in each of the following words in order to arrive at a new meaningful word. Start from the first alphabet only after you attempt it.

Maid (Example)	Raid	Rain	Ran	Rin	
Bun					
South					
Invert					
Post					
Fine					
Fix					
Dear					
Crack					
Mate					
Plane					
Rose					
Pine					

Tips: Application of vocabulary memory, sequential reasoning and reconstruction of words.

13.17: Learn a Foreign Language

Learning a foreign language is a good method that one can use to practise techniques in improving the memory. Learning a new set of words is often a matter of association of a nonsensical set of syllables with a counterpart in your own language.

Normally, most people have related foreign words by repeating it over and over again. You can improve this laborious way of learning by using two main techniques: basic mnemonics and town language mnemonics.

13.17.1: Basic mnemonics

This is a very simple way of using the association method. You can use images to link a word or phrase in your own language and its counterpart in the foreign one.

Here is an example of learning English-Spanish vocabulary:

English: apple, Spanish: manzana—you can associate the last letter of manzana to the first letter of the word apple.

English: olives, Spanish: oliva—just eliminate the last letter and pronounce it as olive.

13.17.2: The town language mnemonics

This type of mnemonic technique is a combination of the Musical Walk with the United Technique. This technique is based on the fact that the regular vocabulary of a language relates to common things—things that you normally find in a town. In using this technique, choose a place that you are familiar with. You can use objects within the town as cues to remember the pictures that relate to the foreign vocabulary.

For example, in learning nouns, you can associate common words to the most relevant locations. You can relate the word for a book with an image in a library. Words for fruits can be associated in a fruit stand. You can also find a market inside the town where you can learn foreign names of vegetables.

In learning adjectives, you can relate common words to a garden or a park. Words such as green, fragrant, dark, large, hot, etc., can easily be associated with common objects in the park.

You can also find a public pool or a pond or even people and describe what you see.

If you want to learn verbs, you can learn it all at a gym or a sports centre. Most activities at the sports centre can be associated with foreign words for walking, dancing, jumping, swimming, etc.

If you are learning a language where gender is important, an effective method is to recall it by making two main categories. In one group you can code data on male gender nouns, while in the other group, you can associate information with female gender nouns. If the language has other genders, then associate proper groups. You can associate these divisions with roads, ponds, lakes, rivers, etc. Simply relate the picture with a place in the right group of the town.

Another easy way of remembering foreign words is to memorize the 100 most common words in a language. You have to just point out the most important words that you need to learn. You could also show how these words are related to your own language.

13.18: Summary

Summarize what you have understood from this chapter—your takeaways—and how you would use it daily.

Chapter 14

Stress

14.1: Definition

Stress is the 'wear and tear' our bodies experience as we adjust to our continually changing environment; it has physical and emotional effects on us and can create positive or negative feelings.

We experience stress since we accept it and move along with it. It's a state of mind which accepts or rejects certain things. It is emotional, dramatic, linked with spirituality and bound by the laws of nature.

Stress can be effective as well as harmful, based on the intensity in which it is been taken foreword.

14.2: How Can Stress Be Effective?

In order to complete a certain task in hand, stress can be effectively managed and manipulated.

Time-bound activities can be completed if stress is taken effectively.

Stress takes a role of a manager to complete the job at hand and compels us to act.

It can create new awareness and different perspectives towards life situations.

14.3. How Can Stress Be Harmful?

The immune system gets disturbed due to excess stress. Stress can be harmful and affect the body adversely. It can make us depend on or develop habits such as binging on food, etc., for coping with situations.

It can arouse feelings of distrust, rejection, anger and depression, which in turn, can lead to health problems such as headaches, upset stomach, rashes, insomnia, ulcers, high blood pressure, heart disease and stroke.

Situational Stress:
The death of a loved one, the birth of a child, a job promotion or a new relationship can cause situational stress.

14.4: How Can I Manage Stress Better?

Identify the source and create awareness about its effect on our lives.

Identify the possibilities and probable solutions to manage stress.

Adopt change management strategies to the reactions by changing the source of stress.

14.4.1. Emotional, physical and spiritual reactions

- Understand the probable cause of the problem.
- Don't sleep over the problem.
- Break the problem into small chunks of issues or challenges.
- Address the events in different perspectives or angles.
- Don't ignore the key elements of the issue.
- Visualize the moments within your body consciously. Do you become nervous, stress out or lose track of things? If so, what can be the probable ways to overcome these problems?

14.4.2: Recognize what you can change

- Can you change your stressors by avoiding or eliminating them completely?
- Can you reduce their intensities (manage them over a period

of time instead of on a daily or weekly basis)?
- Can you shorten your exposure to stress (take a break, leave the physical premises)?
- Can you devote the time and energy necessary to make a change (goal setting, time management techniques, and delayed gratification strategies may be helpful here)?

14.4.3: Reduce the intensity of your emotional reactions to stress

The stress reaction is triggered by your perception of danger, physical and/or emotional.

- Are you viewing your stressors in exaggerated terms and/or taking a difficult situation and making it a disaster?
- Are you trying to please everyone?
- Are you overreacting and viewing things as absolutely critical and urgent?
- Do you feel you must always prevail in every situation?

Work at adopting more moderate views; try to see the stress as something you can cope with rather than something that overpowers you.

Try to temper your excess emotions. Put the situation in perspective. Do not labour on the negative aspects and the 'what ifs'.

14.4.4: Build your physical reserves

- Exercise for cardiovascular fitness three to four times a week (moderate, prolonged rhythmic exercise, such as walking, swimming, cycling, or jogging is best).
- Eat well-balanced, nutritious meals.
- Maintain your ideal weight.
- Avoid nicotine, excessive caffeine and other stimulants.
- Mix leisure with work. Take breaks and get away when you can.

- Get enough sleep. Be as consistent with your sleep schedule as possible.

14.4.5: Maintain your emotional reserves

- Develop some mutually supportive friendships/relationships.
- Pursue realistic goals which are meaningful to you, rather than goals others have for you that you do not share.
- Expect some frustrations, failures and sorrows.
- Always be kind and gentle with yourself—be a friend to yourself.

14.5: Activity: Physical Reaction

Learn to moderate your physical reactions to stress

- Sit in a relaxed place in a comfortable position.
- Breathe slowly and deeply for about three minutes
- After some time, you will feel relaxed, since it has now reduced muscle tension.
- Be in this position for a few more minutes.

14.6: Stress Busters

Examinations are very close and the stress has started tightening its grip on your mind. How can you get rid of this?

It is very simple. Just try a few of these activities and you will feel the stress go away.

1. Divide the number of days that are available before the date of commencement of examination with the number of subjects. You will know the exact number of days available per subject. Plan accordingly and in a day, do not try to study more than two subjects.
2. If you are weak in a particular subject, spare more time for it. It is always better to schedule the best part of your day for weak subjects.

3. Have a healthy and nutritious diet every day; eat at regular intervals rather than too much at a time.
4. Avoid having a heavy meal before appearing for any exam. It is advised that you must stop taking anything before at least one hour from the examination.
5. What to do when you are under stress? Sit in a comfortable posture, take long and deep breaths and release them slowly. Repeat this process at least three times. You may try any of these too: (a) talk to your best friend (b) take a short walk (c) play for a while.
6. Always focus on your strengths and ignore your weaknesses.
7. If you are unable to sleep properly because of stress, close your eyes and start counting backwards from 100 to 1.
8. 'Whatever I learn, I remember, and I will be able to recall it during examination.' Repeat this sentence when you go to bed, when you get up in the morning and whenever you are under stress.
9. Do you know what is the cause of stress? Who is responsible for it? We are responsible for it as we invite stress. We do not study throughout the year. As the exams get closer, the bulk of material to learn is too much. Therefore, I suggest learning repeatedly as this is a 'learn and forget' process. By doing so, the learning time reduces while retention period increases.

So, enjoy stress-free examinations and do your best.

14.7: Summary
Summarize what you have understood from this chapter—your takeaways—and how you would use it daily.

Chapter 15

Meditation and Relaxation

15.1: What is Meditation?

Meditation is a process where an individual focuses his mind, energy and attention, and creates an internal thought process to achieve a mentally clear and emotionally calm state. This includes:

1. Journey within
2. Calming the mind and relaxing the body
3. Emptying the mind fully
4. Conscious interaction within the body, dealing with mind and thought process
5. State of live consciousness
6. Internal assessment for making peace with finer self
7. No barrier between the conscious and subconscious mind
8. Establishing a link between the denser regions of the mind and the waking consciousness
9. Conscious approach and deliberate shifting of mind for inner peace

Meditation is a process of shifting the consciousness from self to something else. It is to be treated as a way of life. It is not a question of doing but a state of being. In order to reach the state of being, doing it is necessary.

15.2: Benefits of Meditation

1. Brings profound relaxation
2. Stabilizes metabolism, i.e., the rate at which the body burns oxygen and food necessary for building up the body
3. Stabilizes the heart rate
4. Increases the blood flow due to reduction in the constriction of blood vessels
5. Due to increased blood flow, lactate is produced. It's production is less when one is calm and serene. People experiencing anxiety, stress and tension have a high level of lactate, which is one of the symptoms of high blood pressure. Reduction in the lactate level leads to deep relaxation which consequently reduces high blood pressure
6. Helps improve in psychosomatic diseases
7. Improves intelligence, memory and emotional stability
8. Brings mental discipline, and thereby, improves personality strength with better social and vocational adjustment
9. A meditator becomes physiologically different from a non-meditator
10. Meditation brings far better and profound relaxation, inner peace and harmony
11. The natural corollary of the constant practice of meditation is inner peace and harmony
12. The stormy turmoils of everyday are subsided and neutralized with the onset of deep meditation
13. During meditation, changes take place for the better regarding brain rhythm (production of Alpha Waves), blood pressure, pulse rate, etc
14. Profound impact in curing incurable diseases like cancer. Dr Carl Simonton of USA has cured hundreds of terminal cancer patients through his CRVR Meditational techniques—C for conviction, R for Relaxation through

meditation, V for visualization and R for Radiation treatment

15.3: Types of Meditation

- Simple Meditation—just sit with an intention to meditate
- Shabda Meditation—being aware of the sound
- Chitta Meditation—being aware of the thoughts that are surfacing on your consciousness
- Trataka Meditation—being aware of an object, symbol
- Soham Meditation—repetition of the word So-Ham, synchronizing with the in-breath and out-breath
- Bhaghya Kumbhaka Meditation—being aware of the outer retention
- Transcendental Meditation—a mantra yoga meditation which entails repeating a mantra silently
- Jnana Yoga Meditation—asking a series of questions pertaining to life, death, creation, etc.
- Subconciousness Meditation—saturate the mind with sublime thoughts—repetition of certain quotations which are effective for better living
- Jala Samadhi Meditation—travelling in a boat
- Agni Samadhi Meditation—observing your own body as dead and being burnt on a pyre
- Zen Meditation—being aware of the breathing and count its cycles
- Digital Meditational—registering and reproducing 100 digit numbers
- Self-improvement Meditation—Repeating positive attributes—'I am able...'

15.4: Practical Tips

1. Meditation is an expression and should be taken more as

Meditation and Relaxation • 151

a way of life and need not be fixed in terms of timing. It should be carried on as a ritual.
2. We, usually, conclude the period of meditation with a prayer which directs us on the path to be followed throughout the day and carries the energy to deal with our ongoing problems.
3. We join our near and dear ones in the meditation so that our mind fully occupies positive thoughts and energy.
4. Multi-tasking is not the way of the mind and it should be allowed to think one thing at a time.
5. Meditation is a source of good health and attaining peace in life.
6. Some practice meditation for peace, others for self-control, some for power and some for silence.
7. When the day gets over, you need to sit and constructively meditate.

15.5: Activity: Constructive Meditation

Were you kind and loving towards all?	Yes No Partially true
Were you selfish, dishonest?	Yes No Partially true
Were you thinking of what you could do for others?	Yes No Partially true
Do you owe someone an apology?	Yes No Partially true
Have we kept something to ourselves which should have been discussed?	Yes No Partially true

15.6: What are Asanas?

They are yogic exercises. A person is required to keep the body in a particular position. There are 84,000 asanas, of which, only one asana is sufficient to maintain excellent health. It is the Sooryanamaskar.

15.7: Benefits of Asanas

Asanas cater to the development of both the body and the mind and impart control over the involuntary muscles of one's organism. Constant practice of asanas will bring the following benefits:

- Enhanced flexibility
- Improved digestion
- Alert and agile mind
- Peace of mind is attained

Concentration and self-control brings about nervous equilibrium, develops a sense of balance, tones the spinal nerves, brings a glow to the skin, clears the complexion, improves the elimination of waste from the body, and thus, reduces the likelihood of diseases and also keeps the reproductive organs in good condition.

It retards obesity, removes toxins and impurities, increases blood supply to the whole body, strengthening the heart, lungs, liver, stomach, kidneys and cures all diseases, maintaining a perennial flow of energy. It also awakens the kundalini, ensures complete relaxation and ease, and is the best antidote for the stresses of modern life.

15.8: What is Pranayama?

Pranayama is the exercise to control breathing. Pranayama is a Sanskrit word alternatively translated as 'extension of the prana (breath or life force)' or 'breath control'. The word is composed of two Sanskrit words: 'prana', meaning life force and 'ayama', meaning to restrain or control the prana).

15.9: Practices and Benefits of Pranayama?

1. Mukha Bhastika Pranayama ventilates, and cleans and stimulates the cells and gives a general tone to the respiratory organs.
2. Ujjai Pranayama relieves cough, aerates the lungs, removes phlegm, soothes the nerve and tones the entire system and is good for people suffering from high blood pressure whose intake of prana is more.
3. Nadi Shodhana Pranayama purifies the *nadi*s (channels through which prana travels), brings calmn and tranquility, purifies the blood, activates right and left hemispheres of the brain due to alternate breathing.
4. Kapalabhati Pranayama cleanses the skull portion, activates the brain cells, improves memory and intelligence, purifies the respiratory system and nasal passages, relieves asthma, eliminates carbon dioxide and prevents greying of hair.
5. Bhandhatreya Pranayama brings strength and vitality, preserves excess prana in the solar plexus and keeps you healthy throughout your life.

15.10: Activity: Breath Count

Have you ever realized how many breaths you take per day?

Since it is difficult to count every single breath you take during a day, you'll have to do an estimate. Sit in a relaxed posture. Set a timer for one minute and then count the number of breaths you take during that minute. (When you breathe in and breathe out, count one breathe. _____)

Multiply that number by 60 to get the number of breaths per hour. (_____ X 60 = _____)

Then, multiply that number by 24 to get your number of breaths per day. (_____ X 24 = _____)

Count the number of times you breathe in a minute: _____
If the breath count is between 7–8, it indicates balance.
If the breath count is between 10–20, it indicates imbalance.
If the breath count is beyond 25, it indicates that you need help.
Compare your number with that of a friend or family member.

15.11: How to Improve

If you do the exercises below daily, you shall be able to find the difference within a week's time.

Step 1: Sit in a comfortable posture keeping your back straight.

Step 2: Plug in your ear with the thumb and place your fingertips on the fore head.

Step 3: Inhale in the normal way and very slowly exhale while humming steadily.

Step 4: Place your middle finger at the centre of the eyebrows, your thumb on the right nostril.

Step 5: Inhale from your left nostril on the count of three and exhale from your right nostril on the count of 10.

Then, follow the same count pattern inhaling from right nostril and exhaling from left nostril.

Follow alternately for at least five times.

Step 6: Concentrate on any light object in front of you.

Step 7: Slowly synchronize your breathing with the movement of the object on either sides of the body. Do this for at least five times.

15.12: Kundalini Shakti

Kundalini is the concept of dharma and refers to a form of primal energy (or shakti) said to be located at the base of the spine.

Meditation and Relaxation • 155

There is a divine spiritual power within every human being, which is a powerful force within all of us, enlightening love that illumines each of us. All human beings, regardless of age, gender, caste, religion or culture, are divine souls with spiritual powers. Kundalini Shakti urges to cooperate for increasing the growth and spiritual awareness within our body. It is our own discrete intention to assist in serving for our enlightenment.

15.13: Techniques to Awaken Kundalini Shakti

Kundalini is a symbolic version of the vast potential energy and power embedded in every human being. When it is properly understood and directed to perform at its peak, the person will experience unimagined heights of perception and awareness. All geniuses in this world have tapped this potential energy for their stupendous accomplishments. The following techniques are used to awaken kundalini (potential energy), best calculated only to awaken this serpent power (kundalini) and make it pass through all the succeeding charkas—from Muladhara to Sahasrara. Through constant practice of yoga and meditation, the practitioner is expected to transcend his personality from the grossest manifestation of worldly desires, passions and instincts to that of the subtlest ones of the intuitions, inspiration, creativity and bliss that are the gateway to spiritual emancipation.

Kundalini can be awakened through the following:

- Karma Yoga: passionate desire for creative activity
- Bhakti Yoga: through developing love and affection for each and everybody without discrimination
- Jnana Yoga: through understanding the mysterious phenomenon of nature and with total surrender to god
- Raja Yoga: through mental discipline of following

the path of eight steps of yogic practices. Only Raja yoga prescribes the techniques of Asana Pranayama, concentration and meditation to awaken kundalini.

15.14: Benefits

1. Slows down metabolic rate
2. Stabilizes heart rate
3. Increases blood flow
4. Effectively removes lactates
5. Reduces blood pressure as the presence of lactate is the symptom of blood pressure
6. Improves psychosomatic diseases
7. Improves intelligence, memory and emotional stability
8. Improves mental discipline
9. Better relaxation than sleep
10. Inner peace and harmony
11. Changes take place for the better with regard to production of alpha waves, blood pressure and pulse rate
12. Helps curing incurable diseases—e.g., Dr Carl Simonton cured many terminal cancer patients through CRVR Meditational techniques

15.15: Fatigue

Stress is a part of life. The activities we perform use up energy and produces stress hormones.

Fatigue is the outcome of physical exhaustion and is nature's way of warning you to pause and live better.

15.16: Factors Causing Fatigue

- Monotonous routine
- Partly finished jobs

- Poor reading
- All work and no play
- Lack of interest and enthusiasm
- Pessimism, indecision, diffidence and timidity

15.17: Relaxation

Relaxation is an emotional and physical state of the body. Relaxation in psychology, is the emotional state of a living being in which there is an absence of arousal that could come from sources such as anger, anxiety or fear. According to the dictionary, relaxation is when the body and mind are free from stress and anxiety.

15.18: Activity: How to Relax

- Sit in a comfortable position
- Put on some light music
- Take a breather
- Flush out the toxins from your system
- Sustained physical exercise

15.19: Methods of Relaxation

(a) Progressive Relaxation—When your muscles contract, you need to learn to prevent it and be aware of its presence. Be aware of the muscular contractions and consciously relax the tensed muscles. It should become a habit. Control your tensions automatically. Progressively relaxing all the groups of muscles, contracting them, tensing them, consciously feeling the tension, and then relaxing them slowly. Lay flat on your back from and feel your muscles from head to toe and vis-a-vis. Feel the tension being released from each of these areas.

(b) Differential Control: Contract and release those sets of muscles; continuous writing and movement of hand muscles can help.
(c) Tension in the neck: Raise your shoulders as high as possible, count ten and then release them. Close your eyes and move your head clockwise and anti-clockwise.
(d) Physical tension affects the eyes: Some of the symptoms are eye strain, impaired vision and headache. Relax the eyes then slowly massage the area around the eyes. Cup your closed eyes and splash cold water.
(e) General physical tension: Can be caused due to prolonged hours at your workstation. Take small breaks. Change your activities and your positions too. Do physical moments after short breaks like stretching your hands, moving your neck at an angle of 45 degrees clockwise and anticlockwise.
(f) Yawning and stretching: Yawning when bored helps you to free yourself from cramps. Breathe in fresh air.

Yogic breathing is a three-step process—

- Abdominal breathing: Breathing through your belly is also referred to as diaphragmatic breathing or abdominal breathing. This has the effect of pushing the belly outward. Inhale so that the abdomen fills up with air and stretch downward as you breathe in.
- Mid-breathing: Having filled the abdomen, it bloats the chest cavity, expanding the rib cage and lifting the shoulders.
- Nasal breathing: Breathe in the air having first filled abdomen and then the chest fills the throat and nose and continues filling the nasal passages.

By holding the breath between inhaling and exhaling and by

taking shallow breaths, keeping feeling at bay.

Resonating: After about two minutes of abdominal breathing in this way, place the tip of the tongue to the top of the palate just behind your teeth and join your hands in front of you. Then, on each exhalation as you feel your emotions beginning to radiate, chant Om for the full duration of exhalation.

Of the seven energy centres, two originate in the head and five in the spinal column. The energy centres must all be open and in balance if a person is to experience wholeness and unconditional joy.

An easy way to determine which chakras are blocked is to simply pay attention to which parts of your body tighten, or begin to hurt when you are overloaded and cannot process all the energy flowing through your energy system.

If, for example, you get a headache when you are overloaded, it is your sixth chakra, the third eye, which is blocked.

If you feel some kind of stress or a lump in your throat, the back of your neck or your shoulders tighten and begin to hurt, you have a blockage at your fifth chakra, the throat chakra.

If your heart begins to pound, there is a blockage in your fourth chakra—the heart chakra.

If there is a tightness in your stomach, there is a blockage in your third chakra—solar plexus centre.

Blockage in the second chakra or the sexual centre can manifest as either an ache in the intestine, problems with digestion, problems in the urinary tract or sexual dysfunction.

At the base of the spine can manifest digestive problems or difficulties in bowel movement.

There is a relationship between health and activities of chakras and even in a person's behaviour and quality of relationship.

15.20: Summary

Summarize what you have understood from this chapter—your takeaways—and how you would use it daily.

Chapter 16

Emotional Freedom Techniques (EFTs)

16.1: Introduction : Emotional Freedom Techniques

For Peace, Freedom & Joy

Based on impressive new discoveries involving the body's subtle energies, EFT (Emotional Freedom Techniques) has been clinically effective in thousands of cases for Trauma & Abuse, Stress & Anxiety, Fears & Phobias, Depression, Addictive Cravings, Children's Issues, and hundreds of physical symptoms including headaches, body pains and breathing difficulties. Properly applied, over 80 per cent achieve either noticeable improvement or complete cessation of the problem. It is the missing piece to the healing puzzle.

—Gary Craig, Father of EFT, Emotional Freedom Techniques

16.2: What are Emotional Freedom Techniques (EFTs)?

Emotional Freedom Techniques, or EFTs, are psychological acupressure techniques that many doctors, healthcare and professionals for well-being use in their practice to optimize emotional health. Although it is still often overlooked, emotional health is absolutely essential to your physical health and healing—no matter how devoted you are to proper diet and lifestyle, it is more difficult to achieve your body's ideal healing and immune protective powers if stress or emotional barriers stand in your way.

EFT is very easy to learn, and will help you:

- Transform negative emotions
- Reduce food cravings
- Reduce pain
- Heal trauma
- Manage stress effortlessly
- Positive goals
- Detach from limitations
- Develop self confidence
- Cultivate freedom and joy and much more

EFT is a form of psychological acupressure, based on the same energy used in traditional acupuncture to treat physical and emotional ailments for over five thousand years, but without the invading needles. Instead, simple tapping with the fingertips is used to input kinetic energy onto specific meridians on the head and chest while you think about your specific problem—whether it is a traumatic event, an addiction, pain, etc.—and voice positive affirmations.

This combination of tapping the energy meridians and voicing positive affirmation works to clear the 'short-circuit'—the emotional block—from your body's bio energy system, thus restoring your **mind** and **body**'s balance, which is essential for optimal health and the healing of physical disease.

Some people are initially wary of these principles as EFT is based on the electromagnetic energy that flows through the body and regulates our health; this has been only recently recognized in the West. Others were initially taken aback (and sometimes amused) by the EFT tapping and affirmation methodology.

Psychological Reversal is caused by self-defeating, negative thinking, which often occurs subconsciously, and thus, outside your awareness.

Since the cause of Psychological Reversal involves negative thinking, it should be no surprise that the correction for it is the neutralizing setup statement and affirmation already included in the basic recipe.

16.3: Common Psychological Reversal Scenarios

Find some of the symptoms below. Tick whichever is applicable to you:

- I am afraid to give up my hopelessness, helplessness, fear, dependency, etc.
- I doubt it will happen.
- I am supposed to be rejected.
- I don't trust myself to live it out.
- I don't feel safe while… (situation _____)
- I have to be perfect about everything.
- I fear something like this problem will happen again.
- I doubt that I will really be able to do this.

16.4: Steps in EFT

- Identify the core problem/event/challenge.
- Measure its intensity (crescendo) from 0 (low) 5 (mid)—10 (High)
- Create a set-up and reminder phrase that feels right (be specific)
- Repeat the set-up phrase three times while rubbing the sore spot or Karate Chop point—the plain surface, starting from the end of the baby finger to the bottom of the palm
- Repeat reminder phrase while tapping on each of the following points approximately seven times:
  - Top of head
  - Eyebrows
  - Sides of the eyes

- Under the eyes
- Under the nose
- Chin
- Collar bones
- Under arms
- Thumb
- Index finger
- Middle finger
- Baby finger

16.5: Activity: Identify Your Problem

Repeat the following setup phrase three times, for example,

'*Even though I have this* ———— *(for e.g., bad headache... reminder phrase)* ———————— *I deeply and completely accept myself,*' while continuously tapping the Karate Chop point or rubbing the tender spot:

Problem: ————————————————
Intensity level: ————————————————
Tapping needed: ————————————————

16.6: Tips for Tapping

- Always remember to do the setup first and repeat the reminder phrase as you go through the points
- Be specific
- Watch for aspects
- Allow the core issue to surface
- Persist lovingly
- Be kind and gentle

After completing the setup, tap about seven times on each of the following energy points while repeating the *remaining phrase* at each point.

Tune in again to the issue and notice any remaining intensity and proceed to tap yourself FREELY...

Note: In subsequent rounds the setup affirmation and the reminder phrase are adjusted to reflect the fact that you are addressing the *remaining* problem.

16.7: If You Get Stuck

Sometimes, you might not seem to be making any progress. If this is the case, then you might try one of the following to help.

- Try a different setup phrase.
- Make sure you are being as specific as possible.
- Drink a glass of water. Move around; some light exercise may help.

16.8: Summary

Summarize what you have understood from this chapter—takeaways—and how you would use it daily.

Chapter 17

Musical Windows

17.1: Introduction

Musical windows is a mnemonic memorization system based on musical notes.

Musical windows helps one remember numbers like other phonetic peg systems do. It enhances memory and consequently makes information very easy to memorize:

- Long answers, chapters and paragraphs
- Historical dates and events
- Periodic tables
- World map with latitudes and longitudes
- Speed reading
- Names and faces
- Task list
- Key points
- Statistical data

Aim: To help memorize anything through associations, for example, anything related to academics, digits, date of birth (DOB), records hh:mm:ss, lat/long, historical dates, pack of cards, etc.

Learning objective: Implementing powerful ideas, in close association with Suvi, Musical Walk and a few other memorization systems, enable memory enhancement and consequently make information very easy to memorize:

- Numbers
- Key points/appointments
- Presentations
- Chapters
- Lists
- Historical events
- World map with latitude and longitude

17.2: Activity: Number Span (Untrained Memory)

Read the number in each line and cover with a plain sheet of paper and write down the numbers you remember. Repeat the exercise till the end.

457	....
8230	....
46729	....
837025	....
9280472	....
67839207	....
173902826	....
2815809173	....
85932615982	....
563289540193	....
7256092301871	....
64293760159237	....

17.3: Activity: Alpha Numerical (Untrained Memory)

Alpha-numerical

5B7	....
82RC	....

7P3DG ....
810G9S ....
36WLX7C ....
R59AP3B7 ....

17.4: Who Invented Musical Windows?

Vikrant Narayan Chaphekar invented musical windows in 1979.

In the year 1979, as a student of law, Vikrant fulfilled his longtime dream of creating a memorization system. Vikrant's grandfather, Dattatraya, was born in the year 1899 and and his architect father Narayan was born in the year 1926. They both used to guide him and encourage him to develop new ideas. They would help him with innovative ideas of charts and mind-mapping since his childhood. He was inspired by his drawing teacher Kale Guruji as well.

Vikrant was influenced by the **sargam**, the musical notes. He, therefore, created his own memorization system—musical windows—based on the sargam itself.

17.5: How It Works

Vikrant designed systems based on musical notes (Sa, Re, Ga, Ma), which can be worked successfully with any Indian regional language since all regional languages have similar scripts.

Musical notes (Sa, Re, Ga…..Ni)

The first note is Sa. The second note is Re and so on.

If you notice the table below, against the No. 1, the first alphabet of the letter S is taken, against No. 2, the second note, the first alphabet R is associated with the number and so on.

Musical Windows • 169

Numbers from 1 – 7 are assigned to the notes.		
1	स / S	PRACTISE
2	र / R	
3	ग / G	
4	म / M	
5	प / P	
6	द / D	
7	न / N	
The remaining notes are BETAAL. Hence, 8 is associated with the first alphabet B, 9 with T and 0 with L, i.e., since all the numbers are in single digits (0 base no. is associated with L).		
8	ब / B	PRACTISE
9	त / T	
0	ल / L	

"सा.रे.ग.म" "संगीत खिडक्या" © विक्रांत नारायण चाफेकर (आविष्कार : वर्ष 1979)										
No. #	1	2	3	4	5	6	7	8	9	0
देवनागरी	स, च, क	र	ग, ज	म	प	द, ड	न, ण	ब, व	त, ट	ल, ळ
+ ह	श/ष, छ, ख		घ, झ		फ	ध, ढ		भ	थ, ठ	
+ य						य				
"SA-RE-GA-MA" "MUSICAL WINDOWS" © VIKRANT NARAYAN CHAPHEKAR (Created in : Year 1979)										
SOUNDS >	S, CH, K	R	G, J	M	P	D	N	B, W	T	L
LETTERS >	S, C, K, Q	R	G, J, Z	M	P, F	D	N	B, W, V	T	L
To create words use the sounds with vowels viz. " a, e, i, o, u " + sound combinations of " h, y " / Ignore silent, apostrophes' & plurals										

17.5.1 Practice test

Let us see if you are able to recall. Write either the number or the alphabet below:

T: _____ L: _____ 8: _____

G: _____ 5: _____ P: _____

S: _____ B: _____ D: _____

2: _____ 4: _____ 9: _____
M: _____ N: _____ 3: _____

17.6: Benefits

Participation in structured memory programmes has many benefits for children and young people besides just learning the basic skills.

- **Improves** your overall personality
- Ability to **focus** and **concentrate** increases
- Develops **interest** and **confidence** in your core subject
- **Understands** how to use brain effectively and productively
- **Activates** neurons and keeps them healthy and fit
- Reduces **stress** and **anxiety,** thereby helping in maintaining physical fitness
- **Helps stand out** among peers, groups, colleagues, family and friends
- Helps to face **competitions**
- Can recall easily by applying **systems** and a **process**
- Boost **creative** skills and **imagination** multifold
- Working with **figures, abstract ideas, charts** becomes easy

17.7: Rules

Musical windows are based on the phonetic system.

- Use clear images while forming words.
- Use sounds related to the digits alphabet.
- Use only collective nouns.
- Don't use prepositions, articles and verbs.
- Form as many words as possible.
- Use all known languages for easy recall.

17.8: Activity: Creating Musical Windows Words

This exercise shall help you to create several different words and improve your vocabulary using a combination of vowels and the best fit can be memorized for active use. You are free to use a dictionary, google words, etc.

#	Choice 1	Choice 2	Choice 3	Choice 4	Final Image
0	Lee	Leo	Lay	Alu	Bruce Lee/Lee Jeans
1	Sea				
2	Ra				
3	e-Me				
4	Ma	Moo			
5	Pa	Pea			
6	Doe	Deo			
7	Neo				
8	Bee				
9	Tea				
10	Sil	Seal			
11					
12					
13					
14					
15					
16					
17					
18					
19					
20					
21					
22					

23					
24					
25					
26					
27					
28					
29					
30					
31					
32					
33					
34					
35					
36					
37					
38					
39					
40					
41					
42					
43					
44					
45					
46					
47					
48					
49					
50					
51					
52					

Musical Windows • 173

53					
54					
55					
56					
57					
58					
59					
60					
61					
62					
63					
64					
65					
66					
67					
68					
69					
70					
71					
72					
73					
74					
75					
76					
77					
78					
79					
80					
81					
82					

83					
84					
85					
86					
87					
88					
89					
90					
91					
92					
93					
94					
95					
96					
97					
98					
99					
00					
01					
02					
03					
04					
05					
06					
07					
08					
09					

17.9: Rules for Recall

1. Use more familiar words, which can help you recall better.
2. Visualize vivid images and actions.
3. Use of flash cards can help you memorize faster.
4. Shuffle the flash cards and call out the number and check whether you are able to get a clear image.
5. Practise every day until you are confident and can memorize all the combinations.

   1. _____
   2. _____
   3. _____
   4. _____
   5. _____
   6. _____
   7. _____

Rating: If you are able to call out 50-60 words — Fair
If you are able to call out 61-70 words — Okay
If you are able to call out 70-80 words — Good
If you are able to call out 81-90 words — Better
If you are able to call out 91-110 words — Excellent

17.10: Activity: Number Span—Visuals (Trained)

Now practise visual memory, based on the technique learnt above. Either create a story using the united method or connect with any of the musical walks which you have created.

47	34	98	04	76
56	85	26	87	43
64	45	97	55	06
23	92	76	09	48
27	42	64	93	65

Now close the above numbers and check if you are able to recall now. Note the numbers in the sequence below and then check if you were able to memorize all the numbers. If you make a mistake while identifying, correct them immediately so that the mistake is not repeated.

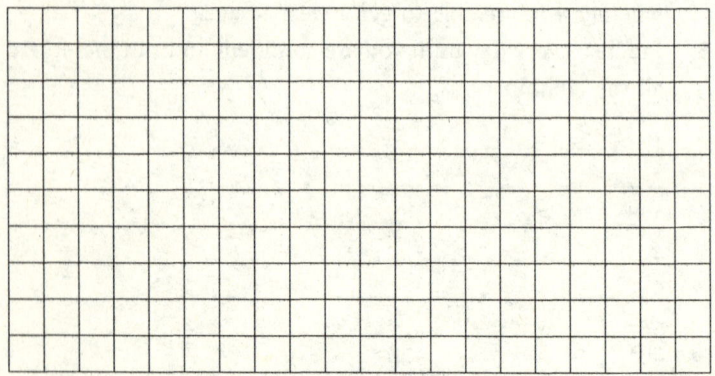

17.11: Activity: Number Span—Auditory (Trained)

Now practise auditory memory: Ask someone to call the numbers aloud. Initially, slowly, till you take a grip of it and then slowly increase the speed. If you make a mistake while identifying it, correct it immediately so that the mistake is not repeated again.

2	9	6	0	3	5	9	4	8	4	8	5
7	5	0	5	3	8	5	3	0	3	7	1
5	1	5	8	9	2	0	1	4	5	3	0
2	8	4	7	1	3	8	6	3	8	2	7

Now close the above numbers and check if you are able to recall them now. Note the numbers in the sequence below and then check if you were able to memorize all the numbers. If you make a mistake while identifying, correct them immediately so that the mistake is not repeated.

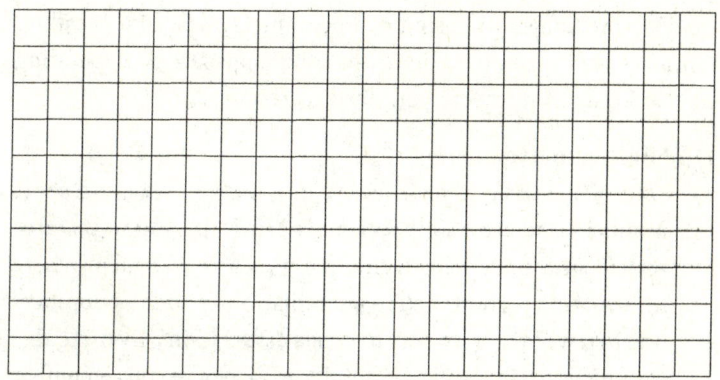

17.12: Activity: Alpha-Numeric-Symbol (Trained)

6#B79
$829@F
#42PXZβ5∞
R734¥€3GΩ₵
6√N37™E№∩6WP1π

Tips: Using photographic memory to recall alpha numerical symbols

Hide the above lines and recall below:

_____
_____
_____
_____
_____

17.13: How to Use MW©

Improve your memory and remember lists and long numbers

Recalling lists are what many mnemonics are devised for. You can retain almost any data into a mnemonic roster list. You just need a bit of imagination to make necessary relations.

As with long lists, using a mnemonic system and recalling numbers is very simple. There are some approaches, depending on the kinds of numbers you need to recall:

1. **Short numbers:**
   One of the easiest, yet effective, methods of recalling short numbers is to use a simple number Musical Window pictures related in a story. This technique uses a MW system where information is combined to a familiar order such as numbers one to ten or ten to twenty to create associations. By using this system, you will recall any fact. It can also help you remember lists such as of the American presidents in their right order in office. If you advance in continuing this method, you can use this to code lists of chemical equations in a chemistry class.

   Long numbers:
   You can recall a long sequence of digits by easily using the MW system. In its simplest sense, single digits can be stored at each station on the journey when you use the number/rhyme system or the number/image method. In a larger sense, you can enhance the digits stored at each station. The number/image method is quite alike to the number/rhyme method. It is an easy yet effective method of recalling a roster or a list in the correct order. It also uses the word system. This method works by aiding you to create images in your brain, wherein the numbers are symbolized by images resembling the number. You can then relate these objects with the number you want to recall.

2. **Contact Numbers**
   Contact numbers for telephone or cellular phone can be easily recalled by relating numbers using the number/rhyme methods with locations in either the alphabet method or the

Musical Walk method. You can then relate these with the image of the person whose number you need to recall.

The Alphabet Complex method is a system that not only uses alphabets but also complex words and symbols, but is more complex than other techniques. It is a better technique for recalling longer lists of numbers in a correct sequence, in such a way that you can describe if a digit is missing. This method works by relating pictures symbolizing letters of the alphabet with pictures you have in mind for the objects you want to recall. For example, if you need to memorize 9#AR@8* you need to create memories of the images. '#' can be seen as a railway track. Similarly, for other symbols, you need to create images.

17.14: Activity: Association (Trained)

Find below connected numbers and associated images. You need to memorize what image relates to what number.

EAGLE	74	BOARD	06	CAMERA	48
WATER	27	MOBILE	85	SPOON	63
MUSIC	50	WATERMELON	39	RAINBOW	06

Tips: Associate images with numbers

17.15: Experience Sharing

Aim: Share as much experiences gained during the training session.

Learning objective: How much one has been understood and how work needs to be done on your creative skills for improvisation of your ability to think differently.

What you need: An exercise sheet, a ball point pen and colours.

What to do: Apply the techniques you have learned in a practical approach and present the same in the classroom during the next session.

17.16: Summary

Summarize what you have understood from this chapter—your takeaways—and how you would use it daily.

Chapter 18

Thinking Skills

18.1: Introduction

Thought generated creates an opportunity to think about a certain idea, concept or any vague, unclear opinion. Thought encompasses 'flow of ideas, connections or associations that tries to transform into conclusion.' Although thinking is an activity for humans, there is no certain formula or definition or proper understanding of the term.

18.2: Skill Sets

Let us now understand what skills are required for thinking:

Thinking skills are mental processes we use to do things like:

- Solve problems: Related to math/personal issues or any other issues
- Make decisions: Yes or no, on certain ideas which we need to implement
- Ask questions: To get better idea or to make concepts clear
- Construct plans: How to execute, e.g., organize a picnic or an event
- Evaluate ideas: Based on different parameters and judgement
- Organize information: How to store and use the information
- Create objects: Best from waste or new product

18.3: Core Thinking Skills

One of the main skills in cognition is the skill of thinking. Some of the key skills in thinking are:

18.3.1: Analysing skills

The first step in the thinking process is analysing. A student needs to think about what needs to be done, create a structure and then start with the planning process. E.g., for a student's academic growth, he or she needs to analyse how many subjects he or she needs to study and analyse before starting the activity.

18.3.2: Imagining skills

Everything we achieve is visualized before it is converted into reality. Our thinking process helps us succeed or fail, either way we are right. For example, when students start learning, they preemptively decide if the chapter or the answers are easy or difficult and imagine the consequences.

18.3.3: Identifying skills

- Focusing
- Gathering
- Organizing
- Evaluating
- Compiling
- Generating
- Executing

18.4: Types of Thinking

18.4.1	**LOGICAL THINKING**	20 MINS

Logic is primarily concerned with distinguishing correct reasoning from that which is incorrect.

What is logic?

1. That is the Himalayan Range. (Statement)
2. Its peaks are covered with snow and it is very cold there. (Reason)
3. Visualize the frost in your freezer, reminding you of the snow-capped peaks of the Himalayas. Connection becomes easy. (Examples–analogy)
4. One feels cold in front of the freezer. So, if we go near the Himalayas, we will feel cold as well. (Comparison)
5. So, the Himalayas are cold. (Conclusion)

This is a logical argument buildup. If we want to win an argument, we have to think logically.

There are three kinds of logical reasoning. They are deduction, induction and abduction.

Deduction means determining the conclusion. It is using the rule and its precondition to make a conclusion. For example, when it rains, the grass gets wet. It rained. Therefore, the grass is wet. *Mathematicians* are commonly associated with this style of reasoning.

Induction means determining the rule being learned after numerous examples of the conclusion, following the precondition. For example, 'The grass has become wet every time it has rained. Therefore, when it rains, the grass gets wet'. *Scientists* are commonly associated with this style of reasoning.

Abduction means determining the precondition. It is using the conclusion and the rule to support that the precondition could explain the conclusion. For example, 'When it rains, the grass gets wet. The grass is wet; therefore, it might have rained. *Diagnosticians* and *detectives* are commonly associated with this style of reasoning.

Formal logic is the study of inference with purely formal content. An entrance possesses a purely formal content if it can be expressed as a particular application of a wholly abstract rule that is not.

In the logical form of argument, for example, all 'As are Bs', 'all men are mortals', 'all cats are carnivores', and so on.

Consistency:
Which means no theorem of the system contradicts another.

Validity:
This means that the system's rules of proof validate the information. It only uses premises that process truth.

Completeness:
This means that if a theorem is true, it can be proven.

Soundness:
This means that the premises are true and the arguments are valid.

The Chinese logical philosopher proposed the paradox, 'one and one can't become two, since neither becomes two'.

The chief concern of logic is how the truth of some prepositions relates to the truth of another. Thus, we will usually consider a group of related propositions. An argument is a set of two or more propositions related to either in a way that all but one of them (the premises) are supposed to provide support for the other (the conclusion), the transition or movement from premises to conclusion, the logical connection between them, is the inference upon which the argument lies. Premise and conclusion are here defined only as they occur in relation to each other within a particular argument.

Logical thinking means constructive thinking

One is the problem which we have to tackle. The second is the previous experiences or previous data stored in the memory on the issue. Information is stored in the brain through information collected, visualized, or by way of auditory sensory organs.

Logic is an important word in our discussion. Logic means reasoning. Reasoning means constructive thinking. The process of our thoughts and actions should be logical. They should stand against testing times. We have to build our argument with solid logic. We should present sufficient data and evidence to prove our argument is good and solid and constructive and our thinking process takes two issues into account.

18.4.1.1	5 POINT FORMULA	20 MINS

1. First think about what the issue or concern.
2. What are the causes of the issue or why has this issue occurred? Think about the reasons.
3. Define the issue. Analyse it and identify any undercurrent issue.
4. Think about the issue by looking at it from different dimensions. Think laterally as well. There may be different effects for a cause.
5. Select the best alternative amidst the many alternatives.

Logic is the systematic study of principles of valid inference and correct reasoning. It is used for intellectual activities. Logic examines if the forms are valid and those that are fallacies. The validity of an argument that is determined by its logical form, not by its content. Informal logic is the study of natural language arguments. The study of fallacies is an important branch of informal logic. Logic plays an important part in life. It is useful in several ways. It increases our memory and helps our convincing ability. It helps our chances of winning arguments and also in decision-making.

| 18.4.2 | **DIVERGENT THINKING** | 20 MINS |

The goal of divergent thinking is to generate different ideas about a topic in a short period of time. It involves breaking a topic down to its various component parts in order to gain insight about the various aspects of the topic. Divergent thinking typically occurs in a spontaneous, free-flowing manner, such that the ideas are generated in a random, unorganized fashion. Following divergent thinking, the ideas and information will be organized using convergent thinking, i.e., putting the various ideas back together in some organized, structured way. To begin brainstorming on potential topics, it is often helpful to engage in self-analysis and topic analysis.

Self-analysis or Self-introspection
Ask the following questions to help brainstorm a list of potential topics.

1. How do I spend my time?
2. What are my activities during a normal day?
3. What do I know about myself?
4. What are my areas of expertise?
5. What am I doing in school?
6. What do I like most?
7. What are my hobbies?
8. What are my interests?
9. What bothers me?
10. What would I like to change in my world or life?
11. What are my strongest beliefs, values and philosophies?

| 18.4.2.1 | **Techniques to Stimulate Divergent Thinking** | 20 MINS |

1. ***Brainstorming.*** Brainstorming is a technique which involves generating a list of creative, logical ideas in a creative and unstructured manner. The goal of brainstorming is to go on generating as many ideas as possible in a short period of time. The key tool in brainstorming is 'piggybacking,' or using one idea to stimulate other ideas. During the brainstorming process, **all** ideas are recorded, and no idea is disregarded or criticized. After a long list of ideas is generated, one can review the ideas to critique their value or merit.

2. ***Keeping a Journal.*** Journals are an effective way to record ideas that come to mind at any moment of time. By carrying a journal, one can create a collection of thoughts on various subjects, that later become the Bible on useful and usable ideas. People often have insights at unusual times and places. By keeping a journal, one can capture these ideas and use them later while developing and organizing materials in the pre-writing stage.

3. ***Free Writing.*** While free-writing, a person will focus on one particular topic and write about it for a short period of time. The idea is to write down whatever comes to mind about the topic, without stopping to proofread or revise the writing. This can help generate a variety of thoughts about a topic in a short period of time, which can later be restructured or organized following some pattern of arrangement.

4. ***Mind or Subject Mapping.*** Mind or subject mapping involves putting ideas you have brainstormed in the form of a visual map or picture that shows the relationships among these ideas. One starts with a central idea or topic, and then draws branches off the main topic which represent different parts

or aspects of the main topic. This creates a visual image or 'map' of the topic which the writer can use to develop the topic further. For example, a topic may have four different branches (sub-topics), and each of those four branches may have two branches of its own (sub-topics of the sub-topic) Note: This includes both divergent and convergent thinking.

18.5: Analysis

Ask the following questions to help narrow down and refine a broad topic into a specific, focussed one. Substitute your topic for the word *'something.'*

Something is replaced with _____

1. How would you describe *something*?
2. What are the causes of *something*?
3. What are the effects of *something*?
4. What is important about *something*?
5. What are the smaller parts that comprise *something*?
6. How has *something* changed? Why are those changes important?
7. What is known and unknown about *something*?
8. What category of ideas or objects does *something* belong to?
9. Is *something* good or bad? Why?
10. What suggestions or recommendations would you make about *something*?
11. What are the different aspects of *something* you can think of?

18.6: Activity: What if...?

What if schools allow students to prepare and learn from home?
Advantages for students:

Advantages for parents:
Advantages for school:
Disadvantages for students:
Disadvantages for parents:
Disadvantages for school:

18.7: Summary

Summarize what you have understood from this chapter—your takeaways—and how you would use it daily.

Chapter 19

Boost Your Brain Power

19.1: Introduction

We need to know and learn how to utilize the brain and mind powers. Science has advanced exponentially and a lot of research been done on how to effectively and efficiently use the powers within to improvise on our day to day activities. We have limitless mind and brain powers within us. During a television interview Albert Einstein, one of the most brilliant minds, jokingly claimed that he utilizes only around 10 per cent of his mind. You have to constantly and consciously enhance the amount of brains that you use. A balanced diet, particularly vitamins and Omega 3 help take up to maintain a healthy brain.

19.2: The Laws of Learning

19.2.1: The law of comprehension

The better we understand, the better we learn. Knowledge should be supported by comprehension, enabling one to recall better, which is the ultimate goal to be achieved.

19.2.2: The law of spaced learning

Learning at regular and planned intervals can help your brain to create a smooth pattern of gaining knowledge, comprehending properly, storing information and recalling when the need arises.

Regular intervals help our mind judge the information flow and maintain them for future use.

19.2.3: The law of recitation

Recite aloud at frequent intervals. Instead of re-reading, recite to yourself what you have learnt. Interrupt your reading and mentally recapitulate the main points.

Why read aloud?

- Improves pronunciation
- Helps to understand better
- Can remain active
- Tone and pitch can help in easy recall
- Can help tuned to interesting rhyme
- Activates auditory memory

Reading aloud and re-reading are not the best methods of study. It uses only eyes and ears. The best way to get maximum benefit from reading aloud is to teach or discuss with other students.

19.2.4: The law of over learning

It is perhaps similar to reciting or repeating the information. Over-learning implies learning the same thing again and again unless and until you get a closer meaning of what you are learning for better understanding. Over-learning helps you to dig the information learned and connect with your learning and experiences.

19.2.5: The law of whole learning

Some students can connect the information faster. Whole learning is a process whereby the information to be learned is connected by a link and you can digest the contents in one go without breaking the link. This helps to associate very fast and enables quick recall during exams. For example, when we have to memorize a shlok, poem or a mantra, we can recite them together in one go for future recall.

19.2.6: The law of confidence

If one learns with interest, passion and concentration, the information gets connected and is stored properly in the right compartment with the help of brain cells. Building a structure of trust helps your brain cells to hold the information strongly and supports to recall them when the need arises, for example, when the teacher asks verbal questions in the classroom or during a viva or test paper. Law of confidence states that if you trust your neurons, i.e., cells, they shall support you when needed. Positive affirmative commands motivate them to hold the information strongly for use at an appropriate time. Doubt or stress releases the bond between two neurons leading to forgetfulness and loss of information.

19.2.7: The Law of reintegration

We remember better if certain pre-defined conditions are installed at the time of learning. For example, the place we sit, the time at which we study. This helps remembering information better. For example, Foreign language is best learned by living in that country, as the environment and people speaking the same language helps to connect and remember easily.

19.2.8: The law of fixed design

Education system teaches us to mark the headings in bold, examples in italic and the most important information or words in a coloured font. We form our own rules suitable for our understanding, which helps in our learning process. These fixed mindsets help us learn the information without even being conscious of it.

19.2.9: The law of unconscious learning

Learning happens with a conscious effort. Our brain, mind, environment etc., are put to work for better comprehension. During the transition from consciousness to unconsciousness i.e., from the stage of waking to the sleeping stage the information gets connected unconsciously and the subconscious mind recites and repeats the information again and again. During this process, learning takes place which helps the conscious mind in remembering information. Positive affirmative commands or instructions such as ordering the mind to learn the difficult chapter or answer before going for sleep helps to repeat them and memorize faster.

19.2.10: The law of connections

Anything that connects or associates helps recall for a longer duration of time. Association is connecting links between the information to be recalled and the supportive means or ways to recall the information. Association plays a vital role in creative memory. Our mind has the tendency to associate the new material with the experiences and the learning, which were similar for analysis or for taking any decisions. For example, if the student finds an answer difficult, he searches for the ways and means he learned difficult answers previously and connects or associates with the techniques or systems in which he had learned the subject.

19.3: Tips

1. A positive and well-directed mental attitude at all times.
2. Deep concentration stimulates the mind.
3. Exercises of creativity and imagination improve the power of mind.
4. Reflexology stimulates the right and left.
5. Observe brain rhythms: Take a twenty-minute break for every 90–120 mins of mental work.
6. Aware and beware technique enhances brainpower and reduces mental fatigue considerably.
7. Physical exercise, particularly yogic asanas, is vital for brainpower development.
8. Spend time in open spaces and with nature amongst plants—it refreshes the mind and also stimulates the processes of the mind.
9. A clogged intestine means a clogged mind. Take care of your diet and avoid constipation.

19.4: Study Process for Final Exams

Here, we offer you preparatory steps to follow for your final exams.

1. **Read:** Follow a structured way of reading. The first reading should be just a glance at the chapter to understand the topic. The second reading should be slow and steady to grasp the information and learn the concepts thoroughly. The third reading is to note down probable questions and answers you need to learn for your exams.
2. **Recapture:** While reading whatever you have captured needs to be reinstalled and hence, you need to re-read again and again to memorize better.
3. **Regenerate:** Imagination can help transform words into pictures. Regeneration of ideas, thoughts and concepts can

make a huge difference in the recall process.
4. **Review:** To mark the importance of answers, you need to review them and confirm the importance by marking with underlines or circle them for future use. Symbols or creative art can help to review the appropriate words.
5. **Recall:** To recall better, it needs to be stored in a structured format. Repetition after a fixed interval of time can help to recall better.
6. **Recollect:** Confirmation process to understand that whatever has been learnt is being stored properly.
7. **Reproduce:** Strong connections help us visualize the information accurately at the right time. During exams, a student can recall the markings, creative drawings, symbols, etc.

19.5: How to Get Good Sleep

Good sleep is essential for energizing your brain, mind and soul. Your thoughts, good or bad, decide your level of sleep. At least 4-6 hours of sleep is necessary for a student to generate the power of intelligence, socializing, communication, listening and concentration to comprehend better and recall things. There are things you can do to get a restful night's sleep.

19.5.1: Sleep at a fixed time

Your biorhythmic cycle is scheduled to get your job done and keep you busy with various tasks throughout the day. If you sleep at a fixed time, your sleep cycle of four to six hours gets completed and you feel fresh to carry on your activities throughout the day. Sleeping helps you maintain your body temperature, relaxes the mind, activates ad charges the brain cells to become more productive.

19.5.2: Take naps at regular intervals

If you feel giddy while studying or if your sleep hours are not completed, you may feel uneasy. Take a short nap, which will help you to complete your sleeping time cycle and regenerate your thoughts and feelings and become energetic. This shall help you to smoothly study later with better understanding. It will also help you memorize what you have studied.

19.5.3: Exercise regularly

Regular exercise is recommended to help you sleep well, but the timing of the workout is important. Exercising in the morning can help to keep your body fit. If you exercise during late evenings, it shall help you get a good night's sleep as your body is stressed out and needs rest for re-energizing itself.

19.5.4: Develop sleep rituals

Your body provides you with an alarm system to slow down and sleep. Listen to relaxing music, read something soothing for fifteen minutes, have a cup of caffeine-free tea, do relaxation exercises and get to sleep.

19.7.5: Make sure your bed and bedroom are quiet and comfortable

The environment around matters a lot while you rest. A sound sleep in a clean, quiet and comfortable room helps relax your body. Clean bedsheets help keep your mind, body and soul peaceful—feelings which help your body reach beta level in no time, helping you in turn to do meditation frequently for a deep dreamless sleep.

19.5.6: Stay away from caffeine, nicotine and alcohol

Caffeine and nicotine are stimulants that interfere with your ability to fall asleep.

Coffee, tea, cola, cocoa, chocolate and some prescription and non-prescription drugs contain caffeine. Cigarettes and some drugs contain nicotine. Alcohol may seem to help you fall sleep in the beginning as it slows brain activity, but you will end up having fragmented sleep. Stay away from them for at least four to six hours before bed.

19.5.7: Have a light snack before bed

'Eat breakfast like a king, lunch like a prince, and dinner like a pauper.' If your stomach is completely full or too empty, it can interfere with your sound sleep. Dairy products and turkey contain tryptophan, which acts as a natural sleep inducer. Tryptophan is probably why a warm glass of milk is sometimes recommended.

19.5.8: Take a hot bath ninety minutes before bedtime

Take a warm shower before bed to get to sleep faster. Like exercise, hot showers and baths can actually help you fall asleep. If you often have trouble falling asleep quickly, perhaps a change in your shower schedule can help. Taking a warm shower or bath at night adjusts your body temperature and that may leave you feeling sleepy.

19.5.9: Use sunlight to set your biological clock

Making sure you get plenty of sunlight during the day is a very good way to reset your body clock. The fall time change marks the beginning of shorter and darker days. Since sunlight is needed to keep your circadian rhythms on track, the fall and winter months can lead to sleeping difficulties and depression for many.

Conclusion

I am sure by now activities, pointers and instructions have helped you understand how your mind, body and brain are in synchronization with each other. The main source of information and learning take place at the centre of the brain. If you can understand the different compartments of the brain, it can help you think better, analyse well and make better decisions.

I wish all the readers a happy and energetic brain. Love your brain and improve your memory for better performance in academics, professional and spiritual life ahead. I thank all those who have been a part of my journey and inspired me to write this book for the benefit of present and future generations ahead.

Acknowledgements

I am extremely thankful to god for giving me this life, my parents, grandparents, especially my father Prakash Hari Mysorekar and my mother Shailaja Prakash Mysorekar (now resting in peace). My family—my beloved wife Madhuri, my elder son Chinmay and my younger son Soham—without whom I would not have been able to move ahead in life.

I would also like to thank my friends, mentors, Vikrant Narayan Chaphekar without whom I am incomplete. Francis Xavior with whom I have spent two years and learned a lot, Dilip Mukerjea, my international partner and mentor in my journey of cognitive coaching, well-wishers who have helped me at every step in moving ahead and exploring my talent and passion of being with students. I also appreciate the support of my younger sister, Shantala, and sister-in-law, Deepa, at all times.

I am also thankful to the following people who have inspired and appreciated me in my training and mentoring journey: Ajay Darekar, Altaf Shaikh, Ameena Yusuf (Egypt), Angela (SA), Arun Chitlangia, Arvind Gawade, Ashitosh Kulkarni, Asif, Bhagyashree Dange, Chanda Surve, Daksha Chitrodia, Dhiraj Badkar, Gargi Lagoo, Gaurav Bhandari, Dilip Rao, Dilip Patil (Director, UoM), Edna Pareira (UAE), Gujar, Hemant Joshi (Bahrain), Jitendra Mali, Kiranpal Singh Chawla, Kranthiraj, Mahavir, Mansi Rane, Mangesh Morajkar, Manisha Dopeshwar, Mohammed Shalaby (Kuwait), Mohan Panse, Namrata Thakker, Neha Davda, Shantala Panse, Shekhar Deodhar, Shramanji, Omprakash Sahu, Pawan Agrawal, Pooja (Singapore), Pooja Durgam, Prateek Yadav,

Prashant Vishwasrao, Rahul Kasbe, Rebeeca (Canada), Sandeep Kulkarni (UAE), Santosh Bhosale (UAE), Sandeep Kadwe (UAE), Suraj Loke, Richard Ben (Phillipines) Loke, Tushar Gawade, Yogesh MA, Zenobia Ba and Asif Ebrahim. I have received huge encouragement from my fellow trainers too.

I am immensely thankful to Rupa Publications, especially Yamini Chowdhary for her timely feedback and Saswati Bora for guiding me from time to time.